STUDIES IN ROMANCE LANGUAGES: 21

PIOUS BRIEF NARRATIVE
IN MEDIEVAL
CASTILIAN & GALICIAN VERSE

From Berceo to Alfonso X

John Esten Keller

THE UNIVERSITY PRESS OF KENTUCKY

Keller, John Esten.
  Pious brief narrative in medieval Castilian &
Galician verse.

  (Studies in Romance languages; 21)
  Bibliography: p.
  Includes index.
  1. Spanish poetry—To 1500—History and criticism.
  2. Narrative poetry, Spanish—History and criticism.
  3. Christian poetry, Spanish—History and criticism.
  4. Gonzalo de Berceo, 13th cent.—Criticism and
interpretation. 5. Alfonso X, el Sabio, King
of Castile and Leon, 1221-1284. I. Title.
II. Series.
PQ6060.K45   861.1'09   77-84064
ISBN 0-8131-1381-4

Scholarly publisher for the Commonwealth
serving Berea College, Centre College of Kentucky,
Eastern Kentucky University, The Filson Club,
Georgetown College, Kentucky Historical Society,
Kentucky State University, Morehead State University,
Murray State University, Northern Kentucky University,
Transylvania University, University of Kentucky,
University of Louisville, and Western Kentucky University.

Editorial and Sales Offices: Lexington, Kentucky 40506

To Bruce F. Denbo

Contents

Preface

This book is not a study of sources of medieval Spanish brief narratives, although for the sake of orienting the reader some sources must be discussed. Nor is it intended to provide a complete history of such narrative, although for the same reason literary history has to be offered. Its principal thrusts are two: to study the structure of the pious brief narrative in medieval Spanish verse exclusive of the Aragonese and Catalan but inclusive of the Galician-Portuguese *Cantigas de Santa Maria* of Alfonso X el Sabio and to treat the narrative techniques employed by the authors of brief narrative primarily in the thirteenth century.

Critics and other students of literature have devoted attention to structure and technique, but insofar as I have been able to ascertain, no one has undertaken to examine the early verse narratives of Spain with an eye to understanding how their authors—men like Berceo and Alfonso X— structured their stories and what narrative techniques they employed, even including versification, music, and the pictorial arts as aids to narration.

Medieval Spanish narrators, writing in verse or prose, as well as medieval Spanish oral raconteurs, employed age-old techniques, depending upon what I shall call the "classic design." This design, of course, endures into our own times and without much doubt will survive into the future as long as short stories are told and read. Not even the new experimental techniques of writers such as Borges, Cortázar, Kafka, Sartre, Robbe-Grillet, Nelson Algren, and others will supersede the tried-and-true, the time-tested success of the classic design embodying nine basic elements: plot, setting, conflict, characterization, theme, style, effect, point of view, and mood or tone. The degree to which medieval Spanish authors devoted themselves to these nine elements will be observed in considerable detail.

The term "brief narrative" has been chosen and used for a good reason. Critics tend to regard medieval short story as lacking in some elements of modern short story. Some go so far as to state that the modern short story hardly emerged before the nineteenth century, at least with the special concentration on economy and singular effects so emphasized today. While it is true that authors like Sir Walter Scott, Washington Irving, Nathaniel Hawthorne, Honoré de Balzac, Théophile Gautier, Poe, Alfred de Musset, Guy de Maupassant, Kipling, Anton Chekhov, Hoffman, and Bécquer lay some claim to the development of the short story, one should remember that many of the tales of the past—in the Middle Ages and earlier—as well as folktales, past and present, are structured and developed along similar lines.

To return to brief narrative, some expression of what the term means in the present study must be offered. A brief narrative is any happening couched in the form of a tale of reasonably short length. Therefore the fable, the apologue, the exemplum, the saint's life, the miracle, the biography, the adventure yarn, the romance in its eastern and western forms, the supernatural tale, the jest, the anecdote—in short, any and all of the medieval forms of short story are brief narratives.

I do not envisage in this study anything like an attempt to prove that the short story as written by the great modern authors—those who follow the classic design and those who violate it—originated in the Middle Ages, but I will seek to point out clearly that all the pious brief narratives penned in medieval Spain, including the *Cantigas de Santa Maria* in Galician-Portuguese, embodied many techniques and structures employed today and more, perhaps, than scholars have noted.

The study of brief narrative in verse treats the genre no later than the end of the thirteenth century. Since a companion study, brief narrative in prose, will carry the genre well into the fifteenth century, one may wonder why I have omitted the verse fables of the fourteenth-century *Libro de Buen Amor* of the Archpriest of Hita in the present study. The answer lies in the content of his brief narratives. Juan Ruiz's brief narratives are not of the pious type and have therefore been excluded. His brief narratives deserve a study of their own.

Introduction

In order to study the rise and development of brief narrative, especially of a bygone age, one must base the investigation upon surviving written documents such as collections of short stories, repositories of exempla, long works in which brief narratives are interlarded (novelesque pieces and epic or epico-narrative poems), sermons, tracts of various sorts, and even history and law. Also to be considered are songs, paintings and miniatures, sculptures, carvings in wood and ivory and other materials, figures molded or cast in metals, and, in the latest stages of European brief narrative as printing dawned, woodcuts and other sorts of printed illustration. Folktales and folk songs in the past were numerous, but one cannot turn to these except as they have been preserved in not-very-folkloristic forms in the aforesaid media and in their survivals in certain areas of present-day folklore. Virtually no poet or storyteller who wrote was willing or even able to play the role that a collector plays today, that is, to set down oral tales in the exact words of the informant. Writers are grammatical, or purport to be, and folk singers and tellers of tales generally are not. Writers, especially those who would employ tales for a didactic or religious purpose, have a tendency to alter an oral tale to make it fit the pattern of their texts or to conform to the special needs of the lessons they attempt to teach. Folktales, then, as they have come to us from the past are not couched in the exact mold in which they were originally told. Their pristine, popular form was not of much concern to writers, and indeed, writers often actually scorned the oral account and did all they could to turn such an account into a literary and polished piece.

Even so, scholars today frequently see in a tale written in medieval Latin or in some medieval vernacular, what a medieval folktale, whether in Latin or in a vernacular, must have been like. This can also come about in the case of a story written in the classical languages, but not often with the same reliability. The ancients—authors like Phaedrus and Virgil and

Horace, and even such writers as Homer and Apuleius who were definitely inclined toward folklore made good use of folktales and folk motifs; but all too often as they wrote they converted these into literary tales and surrounded them with the aura of ancient myths which had long been handled literarily. Whether, then, we are dealing with classical tales, which themselves probably originated in preclassical popular or oral tales, or with medieval tales of similar origin, it is sometimes possible to posit, through the study of modern folktales, what a folktale might have been like in, say, the Age of Augustus or of Alfonso el Sabio. To some extent Homer, especially in the *Odyssey,* is closer to the mainsprings of oral folktales than one might suspect. When his masterpieces were finally written down, many Greeks were unable to read. Therefore his works had to be read aloud or recited, for otherwise many of his contemporaries could never have delighted in his epics, nor have been instructed by them. Since scholars now believe that all Ancient Hellas and her colonies knew and loved Homeric works, they must accept the certainty of oral representation and transmission.[1]

With Apuleius, often considered the most representative in the use of folk materials, it is not the same. While he borrowed from folklore, as well as from the myths which had long since become literature, he wrote for a reading public, and it is doubtful that the inimitable tales as written in the *Golden Ass* ever rang through the huts of shepherds or across the decks of ships at sea. The folktales used by him, and by Homer, needless to say, were alive in parallel popular versions. Indeed, some have survived the ages in oral transmission; but it was Homer, not Apuleius, who aimed his opus at the illiterate as well as the literate. In any case, if we could not study in living folktales the analogues of ancient myths or mythic tales, we could hardly have any idea as to the composition of ancient stories.

To return to medieval brief narratives found in books or in other media, it should be made clear why it is easier to re-create their pristine form than it is to do so in the case of tales from antiquity. One reason is that the medieval analogues in current folktales can be more readily seen. These analogues enable us to trace the origins of many stories, otherwise unidentifiable. For various reasons in the Middle Ages—social, religious, cultural—new and quite different types of tales rose to the surface, some from the most ancient folklores of Europe, and from such popular lore literary tales were created. In Spain, but also in other areas, the ancestral lore was closer to the people than were the myths and legends handed down from pagan antiquity. Remarkably interesting cycles of indigenous folktales, cast into literary form, exist and have exercised an almost phenomenal influence upon medieval literatures surviving into modern times as novels, operas, concerts, ballets, paintings, sculptures, etc. In areas beyond the Pyrenees, and to a lesser extent in the Iberian Peninsula, the whole world of Arthurian Romance, with the cycle of the Holy Grail, the tales of Marie de France and of Chrestian de Trois, to name but two, contributed. Analogues between such examples as the Swan Knight and certain surviving folktales have been discovered, as have those between the legends of Tristan and Isolde, and similar tales still are told today in places as far apart as Ireland and Macedonia or Spain and Appalachia.[2]

The myths of ancient times, then, were not in the ken of most medieval people and were familiar principally to those who could read—schoolmen, students, theologians, and legists. If myths survived into the times of Juan Ruiz, they appeared in altered form and were often presented for new reasons. Even Aesop's *Fables* which could be told as they had been originally, but in vernacular tongues, were slanted to give moralizations not always in keeping with their originals.

To replace the myths that had been the cornerstone of ancient pagan religions and literatures, the Church turned to less venerable sources for its own mythology.[3] It turned to the legends of its own heroes and heroines, to its martyrs and its saints, to the Blessed Virgin and her Son, and to their adversaries, the devil and his imps, the incubi and succubi, the witches and warlocks, and to the many beastly and supernatural denizens of post-classical times as well as to the supernatural elements imported from the East. It is in the popularization of age-old, as well as of current, subject matter that we can recognize among the folk the presence of narrative traditions and legends quite as old or even older than the superstitions and legends of the Ancient World, and yet these narratives are more pertinent and more receptive to the medieval mind. It is not strange that so many have survived and have analogues, sometimes in surprisingly faithful form, even to certain linguistic archaisms, in present-day tales taped by folklorists in the slums of Los Angeles and Madrid.

Another reason for analogues, especially in Spain, but also in other European lands, is the presence of the Christian faith. Written at first in medieval Latin and then in the vernaculars of all countries, such tales could hardly die, for the Church perpetuated them. Some came straight from oral tradition or folklore and entered the collections of exempla in almost pristine form, while others considered as eyewitness accounts were included; still others, garnered from older collections like the *Vitae Patrum,* from the works of Rabanus Maurus, the Venerable Bede, Braulius, Isidore, Notker, and Ehrismann, blossomed and flourished in the medieval languages spoken by the people. The results can be read in the *Fabulae* of Odo of Cheriton, of which there was a Spanish version, and the masterpieces of Alfonso el Sabio, Gonzalo de Berceo, Juan Ruiz, and Don Juan Manuel, some of which were pietistic in nature and some of secular nature.

Still another important source, which actually was a combination of many sources, was the material that was brought home by returning crusaders and by merchants whose interest in the West had been aroused in the East by the many Christians in all ranks of society. Eastern books were brought in as well as oral tales to thrill the medieval mind with their content, much of which was new.

Apart from the pietistic tales espoused by the Church in its western and its eastern branches, considerable in the form of collections of tales, many of entirely secular eastern origin, made their appearance in Europe. Spain was the recipient of many, both of novelesque and briefer character. But many of the same eastern repositories found their way into France, Italy, and even to such northern lands as the British Isles, Germany, and Scandinavia.

The folk of Europe eventually received these tales, even if the books which contained them remained in the province of erudite and courtly circles, for stories have a way of filtering down from the school and the court to the street and the pasture. Nor must one forget the itinerant preachers, as well as the itinerant professional taletellers. Both groups wended their way across the continent. The richness of it all staggers the mind, and it is therefore difficult to choose a place of beginning or an exact time. But since the Spanish brief narrative, both in prose and in verse, generally follows pan-European traditions and has similar origins, similar reasons for being, the same aims and goals, approaches and structures, it seems relevant, as regards Spain, to examine first the potential of folkloric contributions, insofar as this is feasible, and then to proceed to other media which preserved stories, and finally touch upon the richest sources in the literary monuments which have survived and which contain most of what can be examined concretely in such a study as this.

The world of visualized brief narrative—in stained glass, carvings, etc.—save for some treatment of the miniatures in the *Cantigas de Santa Maria,* must be set aside insofar as this volume and its prospective companion, *Brief Narrative in Medieval Spanish Prose,* are concerned.

The Folktale and Its Contributions

Since any history of a literary genre, such as the brief narrative, must take into account the folktale simply because folktales have existed from the beginning and have been the fundamental step in the development of brief narrative everywhere, some effort must be made to understand the richness of folklore as a background of medieval brief narrative. But, since the history of the folktale depends so heavily upon supposition and theory, the folktale can only form a subsidiary part of this overall consideration of brief narrative.

Folktales existed in the Iberian Peninsula quite probably from the time men there were capable of communication. How can we believe otherwise from what we know of the rise and development of brief narrative across the entire earth? How could we entertain the thought that a similar development did not occur in the area we know as Spain and Portugal? Folktales were surely told there, and no doubt for the same reasons they have been told and are being told elsewhere—for reasons recreational and didactic. Within these two spectra all varieties of tales can be placed. Stories that delight, titillate, frighten, puzzle, uplift—indeed the list could be greatly expanded—have always been told; and stories that teach, guide, reveal, interpret, or explain the meanings of things in nature, the world, the universe, and the cosmos themselves have always existed. Rare is the story, even in our more sophisticated times, the mood piece, the impressionistic tale, the slice of life that does not seek to entertain or interest or in some way, at the same time, to instruct.

Scholars know very little about the preclassical inhabitants of the Peninsula. The Iberians wrote, the Celts did not, and of other almost legendary peoples even less is known. Later came the Phoenicians, the Greeks, the Etruscans, the Carthaginians, and most important, the Romans trailing in their wake many of the peoples living under Roman domination—Mauritanians, Italians of various stocks, Gauls, Germans, and even far-flung mercenaries from the Levant, Egypt, Abyssinia, and more distant

Asia. And when Rome had lost the power to govern her distant provinces, the barbarians invaded—Alans, Vandals and others, and then the Visigoths who eventually called in the armies of Rome's last bastion, the Eastern Empire, more Greek than Roman, to assist them against their enemies. As the kingdom of the Goths flickered and died out, still another polyglot invasion came, led by Arabs—Syrians, Moroccan Moors, Berbers, Black Africans, and other less noteworthy components of Islamic power. All these peoples brought their folktales, and some brought their literary tales. It is interesting to speculate about popular tales brought into Spain by the Islamic invasion, but we can speak with more certainty about Islamic literary tales. Interestingly enough, the Arabs and their allies caused a kind of revival of many ancient Indo-European tales that might have long since reached Spain and which, conceivably might have survived into the time of the revival under the Moslems. I mean, of course, the very ancient tales believed to have originated among the ancient Indo-Europeans and taken by them into India, where these tales were adapted to the subcontinent. Later, they were borrowed by Persians and then by Arabs, both as folktales and as literary tales. Some of those tales, possessed by other branches of the Indo-Europeans had also reached what is now Germany, Greece, Italy, France, Great Britain, and pre-Greek Spain and had become part of the folklore of those areas. Probably most of the stories died, but many were reestablished later by the Arabs, certainly in written stories, and possibly in oral versions as well.

Few areas inhabited by men have been the recipients of such a host of widely variegated races, religions, and civilizations as Spain. Many of these have overlapped, and their descendants, few or numerous, survived as conquered peoples, to be absorbed into what became eventually the Spanish nation. For thousands of years, no one knows how many, folktales sprouted in that native soil or were imported and planted in it. Some lived, some died, some were adapted to the Spanish temperament. Some tales were changed to make them conform to different religious beliefs; in the late Middle Ages, for example, a miraculous story about Venus would be changed into a miraculous tale about the Virgin Mary.[1] Others were changed because some of the original elements from earlier cultures had little relevance to the Spanish milieu and were therefore not comprehensible. One is reminded of that Sanskrit story of a mongoose which saved its master's child from a cobra only to be accused of attacking the child and slain unjustly. Arabs and Persians changed the mongoose into a cat, for better understanding, and Spaniards made it a dog in one version, a cat in another. In the British Isles, the tale was altered even more, for there the mongoose's part is played by a wolfhound and the cobra's by a wolf.[2] This vast and still not entirely understood movement of peoples into and out of Spain makes it evident why it is impossible to discover the beginnings of the brief narrative genre there. But it is reasonable to assume that representative tales of many of the folk cultures as well as of literary cultures mentioned above survived, if not in their pristine form, then in some altered or evoluted one, to be told, even today, by the folk and to appear in historical times in Arabic, Hebraic, Latin, Spanish, and Portuguese medieval literatures, as well as in Catalan. A substratum, or veins of many substrata, existed in the Middle Ages, and a few stories, not yet identified as to literary sources, or for that matter with definite popular sources, have been found in medieval writings. Such tales can still be collected from informants by the folklorist.

Such may have been the potential, such the intricately stratified lore of brief narrative in the Peninsula. Not much of it before the Middle Ages or at least before the Islamic Conquest which began in 711 can be assessed—not much, at least, save the dusty repositories of classical literature and the pietistic and scriptural tales perpetuated, refurbished, and even created by the Church. Stith Thompson, probably the authority today on the folktale, saw the Peninsula as "a rather distinct unit." He realized that the seven hundred years of occupation by the Moors had left a permanent mark of its own. And he grasped the power of Spanish orthodoxy which reflected itself in the great interest of the Spanish and Portuguese people in pietistic stories of all kinds, as well as in tales of miraculous manifestations. He believed that nowhere do the ordinary folktale and the saint's legend approach each other as in these countries. He was fully cognizant of the impact of Peninsular folktale upon the folktale in Spanish and Portuguese America.[3]

Folktales, then, had been a component of Peninsular life for ages, long before the first written collections of tales appeared in the Spanish language. Ancient and medieval oral collections, and the repertories of professional storytellers, old wives, pagan priests, and Christian or Moslem preachers and others who entertained or taught with tales, are beyond recall, since no one gathered them and set them down for posterity. Rarely—and this occasional appearance must be carefully investigated—did anyone until the nineteenth century seriously collect oral tales and preserve them in writing. As a result hundreds of brief narratives have faded into oblivion.

Folklorists are still busy in Spain and Spanish America, with which we must include areas of the United States in which Hispano-Americans live. New collections of folktales gathered in many parts of these areas are being published and scholars are studying their origins and their parallels in the mother country. The debt of medieval Spanish brief narrative to folkloristic sources may be even greater than has been supposed. Subsequent research and publication will someday make this debt clearer than it is at present.

Chapter Two

The Beginnings of Brief
Narrative in Spain

Before one can proceed to the manifestations of brief narrative in the medieval Spanish language, he must be mindful of the magnitude of medieval Latin literature in virtually all genres. Across the entire Middle Ages Latin lyric poems, chronicles, scientific treatises, saints' lives, collections of fables, religious tracts, hymns and secular songs, novelesque works, dramas, and even epics composed most of the archives.[1] The volume of material—classical, patristic, medieval—formed a vast background for the writings in vernacular tongues. Its influence in subject matter and in form and technique even today is not fully realized. And in Spain until the late years of the twelfth century and the early years of the thirteenth, little literature of any variety existed except in Latin. Then, with the background literature of Latin writings ever present, the first timid beginnings of vernacular writings made their appearance, and many of these were either translations or renditions from Latin models or they were vernacular copies or adaptations of the Latin. Even a Latin version of the *Poema de mio Cid* was written, obviously also for an erudite public, and in it one may see the process in reverse, for in the case of the Spanish epic poem it was the vernacular which appeared before the Latin rendition, or so we think.[2]

The oldest extant brief narratives in written form were in verse and date from the late twelfth and early thirteenth centuries. Perhaps the earliest is *La vida de Santa Maria Egipciaca,* but its contemporary, *El libre dels tres reys d'Orient,* might also claim the honor. Both, as their titles indicate, are pietistic, and both existed earlier in Latin. Indeed the former may stem directly from an original attributed to Bishop Robert Grosseteste of Lincoln or from some lost Old French or Old Provençal rendition. The second is among the most winsome and primitively attractive of all medieval stories. It is, then, with these two poems that one must begin to study brief narrative in Spanish. Both are concise enough to be read at a sitting, even though the *Vida* runs to 1,446 verses, and both quite probably were read at table when such pieces were customarily recited either before or after meals. But this does not exclude the probability of readings by the clergy in church, city streets, and country byways. Though primitive, ingenuous, and couched in a simple and imperfect versification, they nonetheless had charm and attractiveness for the people who heard them or read them, and even today, if approached with a receptive mind, they are rewarding, both in the pleasure they can provide and the lessons they teach. Measured against popular miracles told today in areas where the folk still hear miracles receptively, or even weighed against the miracles read today by students in sectarian schools, both the *Vida* and the *Libre* compare favorably.

LA VIDA DE SANTA MARIA EGIPCIACA

The unknown author or renderer of the *Vida de Santa Maria Egipciaca*[3] was in all probability a religious of Aragonese stock, to judge by the dialectal aspects of his spelling. He employs narrative techniques of considerable charm and skill, in no way inferior to the model he followed, and he injects into his rendition considerable that is original in that it is Spanish in background and in imagery. Addressing himself directly to his audience—always an effective technique—he follows the popular pattern of representative saints' lives. When compared with the Old French version or with the Latin, his work emerges certainly more than the servile translation Díaz Plaja thought it to be.[4] Amador de los Ríos, whose criticism and erudition must still be taken into account, detected a Spanish propensity for detail, considerable originality as to realism, and a definite sense of the power of comparison and contrast.[5] These qualities, together with a greater use of dialogue than is found in the model or models, make for considerable freshness.

The introductory lines, which are an exhortation that sets the tone, assure the reader or hearer that the story will be a true one, that those who love God, if they read it, will receive values greater than from fables, and that it will be a harsh writing for those who do not love Him. These introductory lines are worth citing, for their content as well as for the example they can provide when the versification itself is discussed. They also offer an insight into the manner in which medieval plots could unfold.

Oyt varones huna razon
En que non ha ssi verdat non:
Escuchat de coraçon
Si ayades de Dios perdon.
Toda es ffecha de uerdat,
Non ay ren de falssedat.
Todos aquellos que a Dios amarán,
Estas palabras escucharán;
E los que de Dios non an cura
Esta palabra mucho les es dura.
Bien ssé que de uoluntat la oyrán
Aquellos que a Dios amarán;
Essos que a Dios amarán
Grant gualardon ende reçibrán.
Si escucháredes esta palabra
Mas vos ualdrá que huna fabla.

(1-16)

The plot unfolds logically and with directness and is no less interesting than that of the more widely known *Thais* and is laid in the same exotic locale. Like Thais, Maria reaches puberty in Alexandria, where as an unmanageable delinquent, she takes to the streets and becomes a famous prostitute. The narrator does not piously rail at Maria's dissolute life, although as a good cleric he perforce laments it. And he seems unable, or at least unwilling, to conceal a vein of fascination with her whoredom, and, in what can only be called a pious and ill-concealed relish, a vicarious thrill in Maria's adventures.

Early in the *Vida,* characterization begins and is sustained with considerable grace and realism. When Maria goes aboard the ship carrying the pilgrims to the Holy Sepulchre, the reader is struct by the bawdy naughtiness of the young men who invite her to accompany them. And one cannot but smile at the straightforward, uninhibited way in which the writer depicts such frank carnality and the manner in which he portrays the amoral rather than immoral promiscuity of the young harlot.

Mas de dormir non ay nada
Que Maria es aparellada.
Tanto la auia el diablo comprisa
Que toda la noche andó en camisa;
Tollo la toqua de los cabellos,
Nunqua vió omne mas bellos;

Primerament los va tentando,
Despues los va abraçando;
E luego se ua con ellos echando;
A grant sabor los besando.
No auia hi tan enssenyado,
Siquier vieiio, ssiquier cano.
Non hi fue tan casto
Que con ella non fiziese pecado;
Ninguno non se pudo tener,
Tanto fue cortesa de su mester.
(368-83)

No reader can fail to see her for what she is—a hearty, reckless, promiscuous whore, happy in her harlotry, a profession she plies more for pleasure than for gain apparently, since no direct mention of money is made throughout the poem. Characterization is sustained when Maria embarks in the Holy Land:

Ella fue tan peyorada,
Meior le fuera non fues nada.
Los jóuenes homnes de la çibdat
Tanto son pressos de su beldat,
Que todos ffazien con ella ssu voluntat.
(420-24)

But on Ascension Day when all were gathered to go to the Sepulchre, how piteous was her sorrow when they either did not recognize her or pretended not to as they marched in procession to pay their respects to the Tomb of the Son of God. Here a climax is reached in the plot and the stage is set for the conflict to come:

Los pelegrinos quando la veyen
Ssu coraçon non ge lo ssabien,
Que si ellos ssopiesen quien era María
Non aurien con ella companyia.
(435-38)

The scene at the portal of the Church of the Holy Sepulchre, when Maria is stopped by mysterious figures who bar her progress, is powerful and moving. Her despair and her touching faith as she turns to the wilderness, where she will spend forty-seven years in nakedness and filth as a penitent, is sudden and magnetic.

The poet has never allowed the reader or the listener to lose sight of Maria's personality, with its strength and toughness of fiber, or her tenacious will, no matter whether she endures the disillusionments of harlotry or the greater physical torments of heat, cold, and the perils of the desert. He suddenly makes the audience recall, as he is confronted with Maria's hideousness after years of exposure and deprivation, how lovely she had been, how softly feminine, how sensual and voluptuous. The contrast between the youthful Maria and the aged Maria merits attention, for the two descriptions offer one of the most interesting and artistically handled contrasts in medieval literature, with a truly startling effect.

Early in the poem one sees Maria in all her physical glory:

> Redondas avie las oreias;
> Blanquas commo leche de'oueias;
> Oios negros e sobreçeias,
> Alua frente fasta las çerneias;
> La faz tenie colorada,
> Como la rosa, quando es granada;
> Boqua chiqua et por mesura
> Muy fremosa la catadura;
> Su cuello et su petrina
> Tal como la flor dell espina;
> De sus tetiellas bien es sana
> Tales son commo mançana;
> Braços et cuerpo et todo lo al
> Blanco es como cristal.
>
> (215-28)

Forty-seven years had changed that vision of pulchritude:

> Las sus oreias que eran aluas,
> Mucho eran negras e pegadas.
> Entenebridos auie los oios,
> Perdidos auie los mençoios.
> La boca era enpeleçida,
> Derredor la carne muy denegrida.
> La faz muy negra et arrugada
> De frio viento et elada.
>
> (724-31)

With horror-stricken morbidity one reads other lines in the same tone, lines whose imagery is unusually graphic:

> Tan negra era su petrina
> Como la pez e la resina
> En ssus pechos non auia tetas
> Ca yo cuydo eran secas.
> Braços luengos e ssecos dedos
> Quando los tiende asemeian espetos.
>   (734-39)

Maria's death alone in the desert is a second climax which lays the foundation for a final element of conflict and surprise. Who will bury her? Who will pray for her? And will her soul be saved?—to medieval people a matter of great importance.

The denouement answers all questions. Even the matter of the lion which comes to dig her grave, since the hermit Gozimas who came to bury her had no shovel, is acceptable to the reader, so conditioned is he, so lulled by the pietistic anything-is-possible atmosphere customarily an integral element of saints' lives:

> Quando esto vió el buen varon
> Muchol plaze de corazon.
> Estonçe le dixo: vos, amigo,
> Aquí estaredes comigo.
> El leyon caua la tierra dura
> El le muestra la mesura.
> La fuessa fue ayna cauada,
> E de la tierra bien mondada.
> Amos la ponen en la fuesa
> E vanse dende en fuera.
>   (1387-95)

The reader or hearer is urged with the writer to beseech Saint Mary the Egyptian to pray for him. If one observes this preachment and prays to her, writes the poet, his will be a great reward:

> Quel podamos fer tal seruiçio,
> Que al dia del juyçio
> Non nos falle en mal viçio.
> El nos dé grant partida
> En la perdurable vida.
> Todo omne que ouiere sen y
> Responda e diga, Amen.
>   Amen.
>   (1439-46)

Recited from memory or read aloud, the poem could have been effective and impressive in its presentation as well as successful in the accomplishment of its twofold goal—of attracting and holding attention and of planting in the audience's mind the certainty that no matter how depraved, no matter how lost a human soul may be, even the soul of a very great harlot, that soul can, through repentance and hard penance, be saved.

A more facile versification would have rendered the *Vida* more artistic, but even the rhymed couplets of nine syllables (a count often broken) suffice to carry the argument along with considerable grace and a primitive simplicity that runs the gamut of emotional appeal from the pleasant to the stirring. Medieval audiences were nurtured on such rhythms and accepted them as primary vehicles of narrative verse, both secular and clerical. In a similar form and one even more careless as to syllable count, the epics, so dear to those same audiences, had been couched. Not until later, in the thirteenth century, would the poet Gonzalo de Berceo insist upon the monorhymed quatrains of the *mester de clerecía*.

To sum up, the *Vida de Santa Maria Egipciaca* answers the demands of the classical design for brief narratives: its plot is sustained and logically structured; there is an attention to setting which is laid more by suggestion than by actual description, although description is not absent; conflict is established from the outset and even though new conflict is inserted, all conflict is resolved; characterization is an important part of the work and is skillfully handled, even when Maria's early life is abandoned for a new life with all that this implies; style is effective, since it was designed to entertain and move a special audience and therefore draws upon an imagery and language that the audience would accept; point of view, though omniscient, nevertheless enables the author to use the first person for effect and to permit some audience participation, since the author addresses the audience directly. Also the poet remains at the audience's level and does not lead it along unfamiliar paths. Finally, tone or mood, set firmly from the first lines of the poem, is sustained throughout and is driven home forcefully as it ends.

Even if the *Vida* was not the first brief narrative in Spanish, as quite probably it was not, it is one of the two earliest that are extant and is surely representative of early pietistic tales told in verse.

EL LIBRE DELS TRES REYS d'ORIENT

The second surviving brief narrative of the period—maybe it is the earliest—is the *Libre dels tres reys d'Orient*.[6] Anonymous, like the *Vida,* it is far more concise. The title is a misnomer, since of the 258 verses only the first forty-seven have anything to do with the three kings.

The plot of the *Libre* opens in a way reminiscent of the beginning of the *Vida de Santa Maria Egipciaca,* since the author addresses his audience as though he were speaking or reading aloud, as no doubt was often the case when the *Libre* was presented:

> Pues muchas vezes oyestes contar
> De los tres Reyes que vinieron buscar
> A Ihesuchristo, que era nado,
> Vna estrella los guiando;

In eight brief lines the scene is set, as to time and place, both of which the audience has long since known. In the next few lines the conflict, which the audience anticipates, is presented, that is, the meeting of Herod and the Wise Men as they search for the Christ Child, and the mood is evoked. People would have been lulled into the simple enjoyment of hearing the old and often-told moving tale which was always heartwarming and nostalgic.

As the audience knew would transpire, the kings reach Herod's court as they follow the star. There Herod questions them and sends them on their way with the command that they return and tell him of the newborn king of the Jews. The sequence is told simply and beautifully. A few lines are enough to prove this:

> Los Reyes sallen de la çibdat,
> E catan a toda part,
> E vieron la su estrella
> Tan luziente e tan bella,
> Que nunqua de [sic] dellos se partió
> Fasta que dentro los metió.
> Do la gloriosa era
> El Rey del çielo e de la tierra.
> (27-34)

After presenting the Christ Child with gold, frankincense, and myrrh, the kings return home—"por otras carreras." Herod slaughters the Holy

Innocents with a savagery and detail that is remarkably compressed into thirty-two brief lines. Then, after the angel has visited Joseph to warn him to flee into Egypt and after he leaves Bethlehem, scripture ceases to be the source. The poet then draws upon the apocryphal gospels and legends which abounded and relates a simple and gripping tale, beginning what must be considered the true plot of the entire piece. In terse but colorful words, the poet introduces the antagonists who are highwaymen, whose characterization in six lines makes evident how dangerous they are:

> Encontraron dos peyones
> Grandes e fuertes ladrones,
> Que robauan los caminos
> E degollauan los pelegrinos.
> El que alguna cosa traxiesse
> Non ha auer que le valiesse.
>
> (97-102)

Suspense is created as the poet permits his audience to hear the robbers discussing their captives and to realize how brutal one of the men is. A mood of terror increases suspense:

> Dixo el ladron mas fellon.
> Asi seya la partiçion.
> Tu que mayor e meior eres
> Descoig dellos qual mas quisieres.
> Desi partamos el mas chiqiello
> Con el cuchiello.
>
> (104-9)

But the other robber is of gentler character and recommends delay and a more practical solution the next day, suggesting that the captives spend the night under his guard. He is even wise enough to offer to reimburse his partner if they should escape. Characterization is concise and clear-cut, as it should be in a narrative moving as swiftly as this, and yet the robbers are credible people:

> Oyas-me amigo por caridat
> E por amor de piedat.
> Buena cosa e fuerte tenemos
> Cras como quisieres partiremos.
> E ssi se fueren por ninguna arte
> Yo te pecharé tu parte.
>
> (140-45)

The poet understands the value of the homely touch for effect. The kinder robber's wife, unaccustomed to guests and yearning for the company of another woman, demonstrates all the simple hospitality such a poor creature could muster.

> ¡Dios, que bien reçebidos son
> De la mugier daquell ladron!
> A los mayores daua plomaças
> E al ninyo toma en braços.
> E faziales tanto de plaçer
> Quanto mas les podie fer.
> (128-33)

The reader or hearer unfamiliar with the denouement would have fallen by then under the spell of the plot, sensing that for some reason, not yet clear and no doubt mysterious, the robbers acted so differently. The feeling is strengthened as the good robber's wife continues her attentiveness to the Virgin. She forgets her own food in her efforts to make the guest comfortable, and she asks the Virgin for the privilege of bathing the infant Jesus. The Virgin assents:

> Va la huespeda correntera
> E puso del agua en la caldera
> De que el agua houo azaz caliente
> El ninyo en braços prende.
> Mientre lo banya al non faz
> Sino cayer lágrimas por su faz.
> (154-59)

When the Virgin sees that the poor soul is troubled, she asks her why. The reply moves her as it does the reader, for the woman's child is a leper.

> Yo tengo tamanya cueyta
> Que querria seyer muerta.
> Vn fijuelo que hauia
> Que parí el otro dia,
> Afelo alli don jaz gafo
> Por mi pecado despugado.
> (171-76)

Then, with a gesture typical of what medieval people expected of her, the Virgin spoke and acted:

La Gloriosa diz: Darmelo varona
Yo lo banyaré que no so ascorosa.
E podedes dezir que este annyo
Non puedes auer meior Vannyo.
(181-84)

The last lines are prophetic, since they suggest the result of the bath. Then the homely and beautiful miracle occurs with a biblical succinctness, vividness, and reserve that creates a superlative effect:

La Gloriosa lo metió en el agua
Do banyado era el Rey del çielo e de la tierra.
La vertut fue fecha man a mano.
Metiol gaffo e sacol sano.
En el agua fincó todo el mal,
Tal lo sacó como vn cristal.
(192-97)

When the wondering mother told her husband of their child's cure, he provided food and drink and sent the Holy Family away in the dead of night to escape his companion's violence. And as they depart, the audience is left with a premonition which leads them to make their own prophecy or to prepare their minds for what is to come. If anyone had lost interest, which is unlikely, at this juncture it would have returned. In his parting words the good robber places his little son's fate in the Holy Family's hands and is trustful that their aid will save the child. Some mystery is evident to everyone, some surprise, too, and a new conflict far from resolution, when we read:

A tanto ge lo acomendó de suerte,
Que suyo fues a la muerte.
(224-25)

We read then that a son was born to the evil robber and that as he and the son of the good one grew to manhood they learned the ways of their fathers and slew pilgrims on the highways, until they were arrested and taken before Pontius Pilate. The reader by now realizes or suspects what is transpiring, but the knowledge does not destroy suspense. Both young robbers are sentenced to crucifixion along with the Savior. The robber who, as an infant, had been bathed by the Virgin hung on the right of the crucified Lord and the son of the wicked robber on the left. Immediately the former recognized the incarnate goodness of Jesus and begged his mercy, as Holy Scripture relates, and received it with the Lord's words:

> Oy serás conmigo
> En el santo parayso.
> (245-46)

But the other, evil to the end, mocked him:

> El fide traydor quando fablaua
> Todo lo despreçiaua
> Diz, varon, como eres loco,
> Que Christus non te valdrá tan poco.
> (247-50)

The poem then draws swiftly to its close with an abruptness that is galvanizing, leaving the reader or the hearer with no shadow of doubt as to its import or to the resolution of its conflict:

> Este fue en infierno miso
> E le otro en paraysso.
> Dimas fui saluo
> E Gestas condapnado.
> Dimas e Gestas
> Medio diuina potestas.
> Finito libro sit laus gloria Christi.
> (253-59)

Both the *Vida* and the *Libre,* as brief narratives, existed in other languages, and since in those same other languages many other such tales were known, one can believe that Spain had a similar repertoire. The absence in Spanish writing of those others does not mean that they were unknown: it only means that they were not recorded on paper or that if they were—and this is more likely—they have not survived the ages. Certainly the lively interest of the Spanish people in miracles, as attested by their continued popularity across the entire Middle Ages and into our own times, would indicate that the miracles not extant in medieval Spanish literature were nevertheless known.

The successful way in which the two stories are presented indicates very clearly that the elements of interest and rapport were active concerns in the minds of the poets who wrote them, for the lessons could have been taught in a much briefer and a much less artistic way. The sense of the dramatic possessed by their authors, and the narrative techniques employed, not all of which existed in the sources used, point to considerable sophistication, indicating a good deal of narrative skill. All the techniques mentioned in the *Vida de Santa Maria Egipciaca* are present in the *Libre dels tres reys d'Orient,* even though the latter is much more brief.

Chapter Three

Gonzalo de Berceo

The first who wrote brief narratives in Spanish verse whose name we know was Gonzalo de Berceo. Some people may be surprised to find this author so prominently discussed as a storyteller, but he was indeed a raconteur par excellence. Not only in his *Milagros de Nuestra Señora,* which most students and critics regard as his masterpiece, did he narrate short stories, but to an even greater extent did he do so in two of his saints' lives—*La vida de San Millán de Cogolla* and the *Vida de Santo Domingo de Silos.*[1] His third saint's life, *La vida de Santa Oria Virgen,* which relates visions rather than miracles, does not fall precisely into the same category, although a great deal of narrative technique is demonstrated in this work. The lives of the two masculine saints, however, are in reality a series of minuscule miracles performed by the saints while they lived or after their deaths, and each, however brief, is a short narrative piece.

Often an author's life has little to do with his works. Berceo is not one of these; rather he is one whose life plays so much a part in his narratives that a biography is not necessary to tell us what we should know about him. Born in Berceo in La Rioja, a part of New Castile, he seems at first glance hardly to have been influenced by literature other than the pietistic, and he stands today as the most representative and copious practitioner of this particular art. On every page his delight in his mother tongue is evident. His love for the vernacular and his realization of its beauty and power to move an audience no longer trained to Latin are but a few of his contributions. His lack of originality, and scholars have overemphasized this, lies in the fact that the sources for the *Milagros* and the three *Vidas* are known, although one suspects that very few people in Berceo's times who read or heard his renditions were aware of this. It may be that Berceo's audience had heard some of the miracles, especially those embedded in the lives of Santo Domingo and San Millán, as part of oral tradition, for it is possible that some of these had escaped the Latin in which they had been written so long before and had entered the oral tradition of the region. Indeed, if one goes back in time to the original composition of the two *Vitae,* he may suspect that borrowings from folklore took place then, too. Might not Braulius, bishop of Saragossa, who is believed to have written the Latin *Vita* of Saint Aemilianus (later Millán), have acquired some of his material from the folklore of the region? Might not Grimaldo, author of the *Vita* of Saint Dominic of Silos, have also dipped into the local legends of his time? Quite probably both did so. To return to Berceo's times, a few priests may have perused the badly written and no doubt fading texts of these lives which dealt, in the case of Saint Aemilianus, with events which occurred six hundred years earlier and in the case of Saint Dominic of Silos some two hundred. Few others would have read them and Berceo himself might not have done so had he not been urged to do so by his superiors in order to publicize the deeds of long dead saints. Even so, what Berceo produced had a freshness and an originality for which he is not given full credit. Originality must often lie in presentation, in technique, in empathy, and in language. The ability to take a dead work, such as the Latin *Vitae* of the three saints Millán, Domingo, and Oria, to retell them in a living language, in verse to replace their stark Latin prose, and to do this with verve and feeling, making them come alive as Spanish saints, is true originality. His *Vidas* are not translations: they are retellings, artful, literary in what at first appears to be a primitive way but which, under careful examination, is quite sophisticated.

Berceo seldom alters the plots he found in the *Vitae,* nor does he in the *Milagros* which reached him in the Latin of his own century. Repeatedly he tells his reader that he followed his sources, even when they disappointed him. It is refreshing to read his personal comments, for they reflect a warm and human mind. In *Santo Domingo de Silos,* quatrain 609, he wrote:

> Caetió y un ciego, de qual parte vino,
> Non departe la villa muy bien el pergamino,
> Ca era mala letra, ençerrado latino,
> Entender non lo pudi por sennor San Martino.

and again in quatrain 751:

> De qual guisa salió deçir non lo sabria,
> Ca fallesçió el libro en que lo aprendia;
> Perdióse un quaderno, mas non por culpa mia,
> Escribir aventura serie grant folia.

Aside from the bonds of plot imposed upon him by the Latin sources, he wrote with a freedom seldom found in works which follow sources closely. He is novel in his approach, in his narrative techniques, in his ability to establish rapport with his audiences, in his powers of description, in settings, in characterization, and especially in his effective use of colloquialism, earthy idiom, and the folklore and local color of his region. It is as though the Latin saints' lives and the miracles served Gonzalo de Berceo as the sketches or outlines of the stories he rendered into full-blown literary accounts, just as stark charcoal sketches served the great painters of the times who over the sketches laid on pigment and illumination in such masterpieces of medieval pictorial art as the miniatures in the *Cantigas de Santa Maria* of Alfonso el Sabio. More on the specifics of technique will follow.

It is interesting and pertinent to speculate on the why and the wherefore of Berceo's poems. Why would a cleric write so copiously in verse on pious subjects? Tracts of a religious nature were generally couched in prose as had been Berceo's Latin sources. It is true, of course, that some saints' lives in Latin and in vernaculars other than Spanish had been versified, so Berceo had examples he could have followed, but what of his versifications of such pious treatises as his *Sacrificio de la Misa* or the *Signos que aparesceran ante del juicio* in which some of his best verse is to be found? Perhaps Berceo's abbot set him to the task, recognizing his poetic ability and sensing that a wider and more interested audience would be reached if verse, then the most popular vehicle, were the vehicle. In the case of the *Milagros* and *Vidas* of the three saints it is even more likely that Berceo wrote at his superiors' orders to attract pilgrims to the monasteries or piously to dun the parishioners into contributing the donations they had promised. But would most clerics, under such orders, pour themselves into the work with such fervor and intensity, with such free rein given to concept, detail, description, character development, and literary handling? Perhaps some monks might have done so, for serious workmen, no matter what their speciality, endeavor to produce a good product. But not even devotion to duty, not even pride in workmanship can explain Berceo's art, even in its roughest and more labored aspects, of which there are many. One can read in his verses his love and his enthusiasm, his joy in retelling and bringing alive again the cult of his saints and of the Virgin and in adding his own libation to the flood tide of devotion to the Blessed Virgin which was at the moment sweeping Spain. No writer whose inspiration was only pride of workmanship or duty could have so personalized his work. Much more was required, and Berceo met the requirements. His interest in the saints and in the Virgin, which so colored his accounts about them, moved him to please them by narrating their lives and miracles so that he would be rewarded by them. Not to be overlooked either is the fact that he knew the genuine and deeply satisfying joy every good teacher finds in enlightening his fellows and making them learn with joy; and lastly, probably most important of all to Spanish letters, he wrote for the sheer delight of writing. He never managed to define as poetically as did Poe what poetry is, but he was able to write in a vein that parallels Poe's sentiments. His naive pride of accomplishment reveals this, for Berceo was not given to anonymity. Humility could not deter him from writing toward the end of the *Vida de San Millán* such happy and prideful lines as these:

> Gonsalvo fue so nomne que fizo est tractado.
> En Sant Millan de Suso fue de ninnez criado,
> Natural de Berçeo, ond Sant Millan fue nado:
> Dios guarde la su alma del poder del pecado.
>
> (489)

The literary quality of Berceo's works deserves therefore some new evaluation in the light of modern criticism, as well as in an effort to stress one of his strongest narrative techniques. Are his lines sing-song and monotonous? Is his subject matter childlike? Does the fact that his *Vidas* helped to interest pilgrims and lead them to his favorite monastic houses or influence the faithful to keep up their donations somehow lessen Berceo's poetic excellence? Does the desire to instruct in the *Milagros,* as well as the desire to attract pilgrims to San Millán where the cult of Santa Maria de Marzo flourished detract from the miracle's quality? The questions are specious. Berceo wrote for his contemporaries and not for us who study him today: the people of the thirteenth century regarded such propaganda as pious and laudable, and even patriotic. The debt of literature to propaganda is too well documented to belabor here, but it should be said in passing that scholars have seen nothing derogatory in the fact that the great medieval epics served as propaganda to attract pilgrims to certain shrines and hostels.

As to Berceo's metrical form, the *mester de clerecía* or *cuaderna vía,* his contemporaries liked it and expected it.[2] Therefore, it was important as one of Berceo's narrative techniques. Certainly he thought it an improvement over the *mester de juglaría* which for so long had delighted those who heard epic and other narrative poems recited in Spain. No author would have written all his works across his entire lifetime in a medium unattractive to his audience and Berceo would have been quick to detect lack of audience response, since it is likely that he read aloud to groups. *Cuaderna vía* is a verse form of monorhymed quatrains, each line of which is of fourteen counted syllables with a caesura or division after the seventh. The main stress of each hemistich falls on the sixth syllable. A hemistich may have six (agudo), seven (llano), or eight (esdrújulo) syllables, although the last is rare. It was not dull or disagreeable or monotonous or sing-song to the ears of the people who heard it.

The full rhyme catches the reader up and pulls him along, sometimes with force or even with violence, sometimes tenderly, but its pull is always felt. And the reader or hearer, once he has accustomed himself to the metrics and the rhythm and to a steady and predictable progression, yields to the unchanging cadence and follows the poem to the end. Better poets in more poetic media have used what some have regarded as monotony. One could mention Finland's *Kalevala* in its eight-syllabled trochaic verse, or the *Odyssey* with its six-footed measures of hexameter, or Virgil's *Aeneid* in Latin hexameters, all of which relied upon set patterns and monotony. And, to move into the limits of our own age, one can cite Longfellow, modeling his *Hiawatha* after Finland's epic and his *Evangeline* in ancient hexameters, substituting accent for the quantity of ancient epics. Monotony? Perhaps. But listeners and readers across the ages have delighted in such monotony. Surely Berceo's audiences yielded to his verses' continuance and flow, to the progression along a definite poetic pathway carefully hedged in with counted syllables, with a definite and expected break after the seventh, and full rhyme at the end of each line.

Berceo knew his audience wanted something timely as compared to the epics, something more poetic, and he was led to explain his medium and its value in quatrain 2 of *La vida de Santo Domingo de Silos*:

> Quiero fer una prosa en roman paladino,
> En qual suele el pueblo fablar con su veçino,
> Ca non so tan letrado por fer otro latino,
> Bien valdra, commo creo, un vaso de buen vino.

Berceo was not a primitive to his contemporaries, any more than Homer was to his, for Homer's audiences, like Berceo's, understood and esteemed folklore and legend and the venerable charm of the ancient and the primitive. To savor Berceo's charm and to feel the power of his writing, one must read him perceptively, laying aside skepticism, casuistry, and prejudices nourished by comparisons with poets regarded more highly by some critics. Fortunately, an enthusiasm for Berceo is now returning and modern poets are seeing his works for what they are. Manuel Machado (1874-1947) composed a delightful piece about Berceo and entitled it *Retablo.* He couched it in Berceo's own *cuaderna vía,* and it rings pleasantly in the modern readers' ears and evokes nostalgically a bygone era, just as Berceo evoked the distant days of San Millán and Santo Domingo. It is certainly worth repeating when one is arguing the merits and vitality of effectiveness of the *mester de clerecía.*

> Ya están ambos a diestra del Padre deseado,
> los dos santos varones, el chantre y el cantado,
> el Grant Santo Domingo de Silos venerado
> y el Maestre Gonzalo de Berceo nomnado.

> Yo veo al Santo como en la sabida prosa
> fecha en nombre de Christo y de la Gloriosa:
> la color amariella, la marcha fatigosa,
> el cabello tirado, la frente luminosa . . .

> Y a su lado el poeta, romero peregrino,
> sonríe a los de ahora que andamos el camino,
> y el galardón nos muestra de su claro destino:
> una palma de gloria y un vaso de buen vino.[3]

Rubén Darío himself (1867-1916), that sweet singer of our southern continent, placed "A Maestre Gonzalo de Berceo" in his deathless *Prosas profanas.*

> Amo tu delicioso alejandrino
> como el de Hugo, espiritu de España;
> éste vale una copa de champaña,
> como aquél vale un "vaso de bon vino."

> Mas a uno y otro pájaro divino
> la primitiva cárcel es extraña,
> el barrote maltrata, el grillo daña;
> que vuelo y libertad son su destino.

Así procuro que en la luz resalte
tu antiguo verso, cuyas alas doro
y hago brillar con mi moderno esmalte;
tiene la libertad con el decoro
y vuelve como al puño el gerifalte,
trayendo del azul rimas de oro.[4]

Narrative techniques in Berceo deserve careful study. His first has been discussed, since his metrical approach is one of his most effective. But other techniques are likewise noteworthy. Times have changed little, as regards the presentation of brief fiction. Berceo, modeling his approach upon tried and true media, told his stories simply, graphically, and therefore with empathy. His determination to develop audience appeal is evident, and not only in his use of the language "en el qual suele el pueblo fablar con su vecino." Good storyteller that he was, audience rapport, he well knew, had to be cultivated. Close and intimate contact between priest and parishioner, he was aware, was more than a desideratum: it was a necessity, and he realized that one of the best ways to develop such rapport was by descending to the audience's level. With rustic priests this was always a prerequisite, just as it was with those secular poets who made their living reciting to villagers and farmers. Berceo, therefore, went to great lengths to identify himself in the minds of his listeners and his readers as a simple member of the rural community in which they lived. His use of the first person, seen already in the two earlier poems examined, the *Vida* of Saint Mary the Egyptian and the *Libre* about the Wise Men and the Holy Family, was one of the stocks of his trade as a pietistic troubadour. Many examples of this can be pointed out, perhaps as many or more than in any other Spanish author of the Middle Ages. Touching, and surely an appealing example of this means of inspiring his audience's sympathy, are two lines in the second quatrain of *La vida de Santa Oria*:

Quiero en mi vegez, maguer so ya cansado,
De esta sancta Virgen romanzar su dictado, . . .

He would persuade his audience, too, that he, like they, was a sinner. In quatrain 231 of *Loores de Nuestra Señora* we read:

Por mi, que sobre todos pequé, merçed te pido,
Torna sobre mi, Madre, non me eches en olvido.

And once, mindful of the love people had for the secular poetry of the time, the *mester de juglaría,* used by the writers of epics and by folk poets, he, like those professionals, asks for a reward, not seriously, but with a homely and sympathetically tongue-in-cheek quality in the second quatrain of *Santo Domingo de Silos.*

Berceo's source for the *Milagros* is now known. He followed a Latin collection of miracles rather than the famous repositories like the *Legenda Aurea* of Jacobus de Voragine, the *Speculum Historiale* of Vincent of Beauvais, or the *Miracles Nostre Dame* of Gautier de Coincy, which may have been available. It was simpler to use the Latin collection, even to the preservation, almost intact, of numerical order of its miracles. A copy of the text he followed, probably not an exact copy, but nevertheless a very good copy, was discovered some years ago in the Library of Copenhagen. Even though Berceo followed a Latin version for the *Milagros,* he did not relinquish his great originality as he prepared his own rendition of the miracles. It may be that the depth of his religiosity differed from that of the Latin writer he followed. Or perhaps the fact that he lived a century later than the writer of the Latin collection of miracles and in a different milieu had much to do with his originality. Or his Spanish anti-Semitism may have led to innovations, and his Spanish patriotism may have caused him to minimize greatly any lack of solidarity among the clergy. These factors and others may have led him to suppress some of the passages found in his sources. It is possible, too, that he considered such passages either improper or meaningless to his parishioners. This could explain the suppressing of lines in which the devil's influence seemed too strong or in which the clergy's vices were too degrading or pronounced. But other aspects of the *Milagros*'s originality lie surely in Berceo's desire to lace his accounts with a popular Spanish flavor, a characteristic of Spanish letters beginning even earlier than the thirteenth century. Good storyteller that he was, he knew the principles of structuring a story so as to reach and interest a simple audience. He therefore compressed into the first lines of each miracle the information the audience must have if it were to understand what followed. The first few quatrains usually set the scene and give the name of the place or places in which the action occurs. Likewise in these first verses the audience is given the name of the principal character or characters. In the first lines of Milagro VII, *El romero engañado por el diablo,* for example, even the source is mentioned, an occurrence by no means common in the *Milagros.*

Sennores e amigos,   por Dios e caridat,
Oíd otro miraclo,   fermoso por verdat;
Sant Ugo lo escripso   de Grunniego abbat,
que cuntió a un monge de su soçiedat.
                                        (182)

The protagonist's character is then quickly sketched so that the audience
is prepared for the sins he commits.

Un fraire de su casa, Guiralt era clamado,
ante que fuesse monge era non bien senado;
facié a las debeçes   follía e peccado,
commo omne soltero   que non es apremiado.
                                        (183)

If the first decision he makes, that of going on a pilgrimage to Santiago de
Compostela, seems pious, in the very next quatrain, his one great sin, lust,
is made quite clear to the reader. And, though to the modern reader the sin
might seem unlikely in the case of a man setting out on a pilgrimage to a
holy place, to the medieval audience this would not have been shocking.
This was seen in the actions of the pilgrims to the Holy Sepulchre with the
harlot Maria as the ship sailed toward Palestine from Egypt and in the
kinds of tales some of the Canterbury Pilgrims told in Chaucer's masterpiece. Quatrains 3 and 4 deserve to be reproduced for a better understanding of Berceo's swiftly moving technique:

Vino'l en corazón   do se sedié un día
Al apóstol d'Espanna   de ir en romería;
aguisó su façienda,   buscó su compannía,
destajaron el término commo fuessen su vía.

Quand a essir ovieron fizo un nemiga:
en logar de vigilia   yogo con su amiga,
non tomó penitencia   commo la ley prediga,
metióse al camino   con su mala hortiga.

With the protagonist's character fixed in the audience's mind, as well as
his sin established, it remained to be seen how the sin destroyed him, and
this necessitated the introduction of the devil, who in this miracle is the antagonist. He assumes the form of Saint James and accosts the pilgrim on
the road. Only Berceo could tell this as succinctly and with such empathy.
The "angel verdadero" will emerge as a spurious Saint James a few lines
later.

Transformóse el falso   en angel verdadero,
paróseli delante   en medio un sendero:
"Bien seas tú venido,   —díssoli al romero.—
"seméjasme cossiella   simple como cordero."
(188)

In the subsequent thirty-one quatrains—the entire miracle takes only thirty-eight—Berceo assures his audience that the devil in disguise is indeed pretending to be Saint James, and he emphasizes this point in the pilgrim's mind by dialogue between him and the devil which is injected cleverly into the narrative:

"¿Quién sodes vos, sennor?"   díssoli el romero.
recudió'l: "yo so Jácobo,   fijo de Zebedeo;
sépaslo bien, amigo,   andas en devaneo.
semejas que non aves   de salvarte deseo."
(190)

When poor Guiralt believes and asks how he can arrive at a state of grace which will allow him to complete his pilgrimage, the devil offers a quick and terrible solution, a penance worthy of the times, and one certain to catch and hold every ounce of any audience's attention, even today's, with a terrible and macabre fascination:

Disso el falso Jácob: "Esti es el judicio:
qe te cortes los miembros   qe facen el fornicio;
dessent qe te degüelles: farás a Dios servicio,
qe de tu carne misma   li farás sacrificio.

When the shocked pilgrims, whom he had accompanied, come back and find him lying dead in the path and cannot imagine how the deed had come to pass, they fear that they might be accused of murder and they leave him. Meanwhile the imps and the devil have carried off his soul to hell. When Saint James himself goes to retrieve it, since the poor man had been his pilgrim, the devils with amazing impudence defy him. Their words would have angered the audience and would have made the story more moving:

Recudióli un dïablo,   paróseli refacio:
"Yago, quiéreste fer   de todos nos escarnio;
a la razón derecha   quieres venir contrario,
traes mala cubierta   so el escapulario

Guirald fizo nemiga,   matósse con su mano,
deve seer judgado   por de Judas ermano;
e por todas las guisas   nuestro parroquïano,
non quieras contra nos,   Yago, seer villano!''
(200)

Saint James argues the case, vilifies the devils, and finally says that he will go the Blessed Virgin and enlist her aid. Her decision, authorized in heaven, was that the sinful pilgrim should be restored to life, since the devil had deceived him into believing that the saint had ordered him to emasculate himself.

If the audience had followed the story, motivated by its interest in the macabre, it was rewarded with an even more macabre continuance and outcome. With most graphic realism, we read that the soul returned to the body and that the man came alive but lay as though stunned for some time. At last he sat up, bathed his face, and was himself. Then, with a medieval approach that is truly clinical, Berceo shows how complete the miracle was—physical restoration through divine clemency tempered by the divine decision not to permit further temptation:

Era de lo ál todo   sano e mejorado:
fuera de un filiello   qe tenié travesado;
mas lo de la natura,   quanto qe fo cortado,
no li creció un punto,   fincó en su estado

De todo era sano,   todo bien encorado,
pora verter su agua   fincóli el forado;
requirió su repuesto,   lo que trayé trossado,
pensó de ir su vía   alegre e pagado.
(212-13)

Berceo describes the interest of the citizens of Santiago in the miracle and in the man who had come back from the dead, and later the interest of the people of his own region. Implication is strong that the wretch had to reveal the proof of the miracle.

Most of the *Milagros* end with the reward for piety or the punishment for wickedness. In this particular story we learn that Guiralt took religious orders and entered the Monastery of Cluny, and that no less an authority than Saint Hugo of Cluny set down in writing his remarkable adventure. The poem ends with:

Guirald finó en orden,   vida buena faciendo,
en dichos e en fechos   al Criador sirviendo,
en bien perseverando,   del mal se ripindiendo:
el enemigo malo   non se fo d'él ridiendo.

(219)

The miracle, like all the others Berceo relates, is a well-rounded story, carried along with empathy, and developed with conversations and concise and graphic descriptions. Its action rises to a climax with the resurrection of the pilgrim, levels off with the account of the interest men take in his case, and offers a mild and pleasant anticlimax when he enters religious orders. The denouement is salutory and rewarding. Even a strong vein of humor is present in the violent arguments and recriminations of the devil and the saint's retorts, as well as in the interesting speculations about the physical condition of the pilgrim and the divine arrangements made to permit his bodily functions to operate satisfactorily.

The *Romero engañado por el diablo,* then, is a story rough and violent and rather horrible in its content. Not all Berceo's miracles are so motivated and structured, though many are. The breaking of a taboo set up by the Virgin is the motif of the first miracle in the collection—*El milagro de la casulla de San Ildefonso.* The devotion of the saint to the Virgin led her to give him a chasuble woven by angels:

Fízo'l otra gracia   qual nunqa fue oída:
dioli una casulla   sin aguja cosida;
obra era angélica,   non de omne texida,
fablóli pocos vierbos,   razón buena, complida;

"Amigo,—disso'l—   sepas qe so de ti pagada,
hasme buscada mira,   non simple ca doblada;
fecist de mí buen libro,   hasme bien alavada,
fecístme nueva festa   que non era usada.

(60-61)

But she makes it clear that no one else must ever don the garment:

De seer en la cátedra   qe tú estás posado,
al tu cuerpo sennero   es esto condonado;
de vestir esta alva   a ti es otorgado,
otro que la vistiere   non será bien hallado."

(63)

When Ildefonso dies and his successor insists upon wearing the wondrous chasuble a dire fate befalls him, and the poet leads up to it with sufficient suspense to motivate close attention. We read of the daring words of Siagrio, the new archbishop:

> Disso unas palavras   de muy grand liviandat:
> "Nunqa fue Illefonsso   de mayor dignidat,
> tan bien so consegrado   como él por verdat,
> todos somos eguales   enna umanidat."
>
> (69)

And so, when foolish and vain Siagrio puts on the chasuble, the reader or hearer is prepared for the outcome:

> Pero qe ampla era   la sancta vestidura,
> Issióli a Sïagrio   angosta sin mesura;
> prísoli la garganta   como cadena dura,
> fue luego enfogado   por la su grand locura.
>
> (72)

The poem ends on a note of grim moralization in which are embedded the two themes so dear to medieval man—reward for good deeds and punishment for evil ones:

> La Virgin glorïosa,   estrella de la mar,
> sabe a sus amigos   gualardón bueno dar;
> bien sabe a los buenos   el bien gualardonar,
> a los que la dessierven   sábelos mal curar.
>
> Amigos, atal Madre   aguardarla devemos,
> si a ella sirviéremos   nuestra pro buscaremos;
> onrraremos los cuerpos,   las almas salvaremos,
> por pocco de servicio   grand galardón prendremos.

Such is the structure of a representative miracle.

Berceo's *Milagros de Nuestra Señora* fall definitely into the realm of the short story. They vary in length from 656 lines to 40, and the majority are from 50 to 80. All are presented as simple tales, just as were their sources. Poe would have approved of Berceo's brevity and of his working toward a single climactic effect.

It is now time to study Berceo in greater detail as a *cuentista* and to view his more specific techniques, aside from the metrical, which have been dealt with at such length because they are so important.

Berceo can be seen, if one studies him with the proper care, as a storyteller of considerable modernity, since it can be demonstrated that he possessed and manipulated most of the assets needed for effective and moving narratives: plot, setting, conflict, characterization, theme, style effect, point of view, and tone or mood. All these are demanded by the age-old and still successful "classical design" of short stories. Berceo might have gained the assets by studying models closely and being the "sedulous ape" or by following the instructions of the manuals of style extant in the time.

It has been said that plot was not his forte. The plotting he followed had been laid out carefully by the men who wrote the miracles and the saints' lives he used. If an author decides to use another author's stories and uses them more or less faithfully, then he is admittedly denied considerable originality. And yet not all that is original need be lost as one translates and revises stories from one language into his own. Inevitably elements of the translator's or the revisor's style and thought and creativity will influence his work. Therefore, even in the area of plotting, although he has been accused of slavishly following his models, Berceo's own creativity flourished. Brian Dutton (*Los Milagros*) has made a most valuable contribution to our knowledge of Berceo's originality as he compares and contrasts the Spanish poet's renditions with the Latin sources. Dutton studies Berceo line by line along with the Latin, and his succinct and logical study of comparison and contrast can enable scholars to observe carefully Berceo's style, creativity, and narrative techniques. After each miracle he edits, Dutton cites his own careful edition of the Latin, a very necessary and long-needed asset to scholarship, since the edition and study of the Thott manuscript is difficult to find and is not as well edited as Dutton's.

Berceo's originality stands out in many aspects of his miracles. He amplifies the Latin constantly with details that are colorful and well calculated to inspire interest and rapport in his audience. Of the many examples that abound in all his *Milagros*, the one in quatrain 60 of the *Miracle of Saint Ildefonso* offers a delightful concept not even suggested by the Latin original. Compare his

> Fízoli otra gracia   qual nunqa fue oída:
> dioli una casulla   sin aguja cosida;

obra era angélica,   non de omne texida,
fablóli pocos vierbos,   razón buena, complida.

with the source's "vestimentum quod nos albam sacerdotalem vocamus, ei attulit" (Dutton, p. 51).

Such little touches, it would seem, can be explained by Berceo's desire to reach a simple public, not a public of priests who could read Latin and who might have been satisfied with a literal translation. The material in quatrain 60 is a fine example of effective amplification. Another, and one of the most delightful, is his comparison of the long-buried cleric's tongue with an apple, a concept not found in the Latin (Dutton, p. 62). In Berceo's Miracle III, *El clerigo y la flor,* we read:

> Trobáronli la lengua   tan fresca e tan sana
> qual parece de dentro   la fermosa manzana;
> no la tenié más fresca   a la meredïana
> quando sedié fablando   en media la quintana.
> (113)

In Miracle V, *El pobre caritativo,* Berceo manages charmingly to swell five Latin phrases into ten quatrains. Dutton points out (p. 69) that the simple Latin sentence "Veni, dilecte, et ut petisti perfruaris requie paradisi" is transformed into the beautiful quatrains 135-37.

> "Tú mucho cobdiciest   la nuestra compannía,
> sopist pora ganarla   bien buena maestría,
> ca partiés tus almosnas,   diziés "Ave María,"
> por qé lo faziés todo   yo bien lo entendía.
>
> Sepas qe es tu cosa   toda bien acabada,
> ésta es en qe somos   la cabera jornada;
> el "Ite missa est,"   conta qe es cantada,
> venida es la ora   de prender la solda.
>
> Yo so aquí venida   por levarte comigo,
> al regno de mi Fijo   qe es bien tu amigo,
> do se ceban los ángeles   del buen candïal trigo;
> a las sanctas Virtutes   plazerlis há contigo."

Berceo, too, was cognizant of the usefulness of anticipation and transition, a related phenomenon. An example of the first can be seen clearly in his quatrain 183 in Miracle VIII, *El romero engañada por el diablo.* The Latin had stated that one Guiraldus (in Berceo, Guiralt or Guirald), while still a layman, had decided to make a pilgrimage to the shrine of Saint James, and indeed, thus far, Berceo renders the account. But to add flavor, to anticipate what Guirald might do, Berceo gives Guirald character—something òmitted by the Latin. The audience, as it reads or listens to the miracle, immediately anticipates from the character delineation what can be expected of the pilgrim and this anticipation establishes even some elements of suspense. It is what some today call a "narrative hook," and it is effective as such.

> Un fraire de su casa, Guiralt era clamado,
> ante qe fuesse monge era non bien senado;
> facié a las debeces follía a peccado,
> como omne soltero qe non es apremiado.
> (183)

Berceo also makes good use of transition as exemplified in the miracle *La abadesa preñada,* number XXI, in copla 500, the essence of which is not in the Latin.

> Sennores e amigos, companna de prestar,
> deqe Dios se vos quiso traer a est logar
> aún si me quissiéssedes un poco esperar,
> en un otro miraclo vos querría fablar.

In it Berceo provides the reader with a convenient catching of his breath which allows him to adjust to new miracles in the offing. And in the same miracle, this time in quatrain 513, the author offers the audience another chance to gather its wits, using a technique effective even to this day.

> Dessemos al obispo folgar en su posada,
> finqe en paz e duerma elli con su mesnada,
> digamos nos qé fizo la duenna embargada,
> savié que otro día serié mal porfazada.

Still another good example is that found in Miracle XXIII, *El mercader de Bizancio,* in quatrains 681-82.

> Dessemos al judío, goloso e logrero,
> no lo saqe Dios ende, aguarde so cellero,
> fablemos su vegada del pleit del mercadero,
> levémosli las nuevas do ribó el tablero.

El burgés de Bizancio   vivié con grand pesar,
qe non podió al plazo   al judío pagar;
non podié el bon omne   la cara alegrar,
ni lo podién por nada   sos omnes confortar.

Another technique of plotting of Berceo's has best been described by Dutton in connection with the miracle of the *Romero engañado por el diablo,* quatrain 195: "La copla es una suposición dramática de Berceo, que suaviza algo el pánico egoísta de los romeros en la versión latina, que cuenta como encontraron a Giraldo agonizante, y huyeron por miedo de ser acusado." It is such minor, but all the same inspired, little touches, that enliven Berceo's improvement over the Latin.

Vidién qe de ladrones   non era degollado,
ca no'l tollieran nada   ni'l avién ren robado;
non era de ninguno   omne desafiado,
non sabién de qual guisa   fuera ocasionado.

Anyone can see that the Latin version made itself perfectly well understood, but the commentary Berceo added is most effective in that it gives the reader an extra touch—allowing his own point of view. A small narrative touch, but nevertheless an improvement and a breath of originality.

Berceo knew another technique, one that may have been his greatest improvement over his source, although the sources often made use of it, though less effectively. This is the use of dialogue. It enables him to novelize to better effect than the Latin did, and it makes us realize how much he excelled the narrative skill of the Latin. In the *Milagro del romero,* the pilgrim has died from emasculating himself at the suggestion of the devil disguised as Saint James. The words of the saint to the devils— incidentally they do not actually reply to him in the Latin version, although the Latin author tells us what the devils said to the saint—in no way can compare to Berceo's mastery of conversation. The Latin's "Cur tulistis animam peregrini mei?" is a far cry from Berceo's quatrain 199:

"Dessad—disso—maliellos   la preda qe levades,
non vos yaz tan en salvo   como vos lo cuidades;
tenedla a derecho,   fuerza no li fagades,
creo qe non podredes   maguer qe lo qerades."

And in 200-201 Berceo dramatizes the Latin still farther and through continued dialogue, not in the Latin, makes a sparkling and moving account out of the Latin's less colorful and less dramatic indirect discourse. The omission of a direct reply from the devil in the Latin version militates greatly, then, against its effectiveness. But in Berceo the devil's railing against the saint tightens the plot and strengthens it, through the delineation of the devil's character as he argues defiantly, even blasphemously, against Saint James. Berceo surely designed this passage for effect and for the very special effect of angering and shocking the audience's mind.

> Recudióli un dïablo, paróseli refacio:
> "Yago, quiéreste fer de todos nos escarnio;
> a la razón derecha quieres venir contrario,
> traes mala cubierta so el escapulario.

A few quatrains later he again uses the direct approach, improving the impersonal Latin account's "ipsa sancta Virgo plena pietate iudicavit animam debere ad corpus reverti ut de malis que egerat posset penitendo purgari" (Dutton, p. 88) with his own

> "El enganno qe priso, pro li devié tener,
> elli a Sanctïago cuidó obedecer,
> ca tenié qe por esso podrié salvo seer;
> más el engannador lo devié padecer."
>
> Disso: "Yo esto mando e dólo por sentencia:
> la alma sobre quien avedes la entencia,
> qe torne en el cuerpo, faga su penitencia,
> desend qual mereciere, avrá tal audïencia."
>   (207-8)

An element of Berceo's narrative skill in the same miracle, which Dutton (p. 88) describes as "extrapolaçiones artísticas de Berceo para rellenar el final del milagro tan parco de detalles," most certainly contributes to the plot, for it enlivens it and holds the attention of the audience. If the *Milagros* were written, as Dutton believes, to attract pilgrims to San Millán Monastery, just as may have been the *Vita* of that saint, then strong rapport had to be established by the poet, and Berceo supplied it. Berceo injects entire stanzas with originality in that they contain details couched, and calculatingly so, in a very magnetic phraseology. Compare his "pora verter su agua fincoli el forado" (213b) with the Latin's use of precise and proper reference to bodily elimination. Wrote the Latin author: "unum foramen parvulum per quod mingebat exigente natura" (Dutton, p. 88).

A reliance on realism and the logical sequence of events and the results of those events also allowed Berceo to plot effectively. The Latin source, as it relates the story of the pilgrim who had emasculated himself and died, is no more than factual. Tersely it reads: "Homo itaque reviviscens" (Dutton, p. 87), which is but the barest shadow of the lines of Berceo with their marked realism as concerns poor Guirald's return to consciousness, his struggle to regain control of his faculties:

> Levantóse el cuerpo qe yazié trastornado,
> alimpiava su cara Guirald el degollado;
> estido un ratiello como qui descordado,
> como omne qe duerme e despierta irado.
> (210)

In Berceo's closing passages he extends the very events beyond the limits of his model. We read, "Hic denique monachus factus in supradicto monasterio cluniaco vixit multis diebus devotus in Dei servicio" (Dutton, p. 88), and realize that this denouement is satisfactory, for it gathers together the loose ends of the story. But we have a right to feel cheated by the Latin, if entertainment and attractiveness are to be part of the miracle. Turning to Berceo, we learn that the self-emasculated monk arrives, after all, at Compostela, so named by Berceo, and the reader cannot but feel a sense of satisfaction that the poor fellow, who had endured so much, finally accomplished his goal, that is, his visit to the saint's shrine. But there is more in Berceo. Guirald's arrival was a matter of great interest to the citizens of Santiago, since Berceo, with decided verve, implies events not actually mentioned, namely, that Guirald had to display the physical signs of the miracle.

> Sonó por Compostela esta grand maravilla,
> viniénlo a veer todos los de la villa;
> dicién: "Esta tal cosa, deviemos escrivilla.
> Los qe son por venir, plazrális de oilla."
> (215)

Moreover, once the pilgrim reached his home, his own parishioners were fascinated by what had happened to him, all of which is perfectly predictable and realistic. How cleverly Berceo describes that homecoming:

Quando fo en su tierra,   la carrera complida,
e udieron la cosa   qe avié contecida,
tenién grandes clamores,   era la gent movida
por veer esti Lázaro   dado de muert a vida.
(216)

He concludes his narrative with an entirely new, but logical, statement
and adds one final line, a short maxim not found in the Latin:

De quanto peccara,   dio a Dios buen emiendo.
(219e)

In Miracle VIII, then, Berceo displays some remarkably effective
techniques, but other techniques are also in his repertoire. So far, we have
seen his use of colorful or striking details, his amplifications of the Latin
sequences of events or descriptions, his use of anticipation and transition,
his dramatic suppositions, his skill in original dialogues, and his satisfying
denouements.

Occasionally, too, he changes the actual content of the Latin plot,
usually only the sequence of events, but sometimes even to the degree of
supplying events extraneous to the Latin. Dutton suggests, and then re-
jects, the suggestion that Berceo made use of manuscripts in addition to
the one thought to be his source. More probably Berceo had a strong propensity for creativity and could have composed with great imagination and
originality had he set out to do so without the Latin models so conveniently
ly in hand. As proof of this, we have the above-mentioned facets of his
originality, which sundered the bonds imposed by the Latin stories' plots
and structures. And we have Miracle XXV in its entirety, as will be seen
subsequently. Examples of such changes, though they are minor, are
worth consideration. In the miracle *La abadesa preñada,* number XXI,
Berceo adds to the plot by including an entire sequence not in the original.
In quatrain 509d he states that only some of the nuns vengefully reported
the abbess's condition to the bishop, while in the Latin account, all the
nuns did so; moreover, in the Latin the nuns in a body are responsible for
a letter which accuses the abbess of pregnancy, while Berceo gives them a
character less vindictive in that they merely write a complaint that it has
been a long time since the bishop visited their convent. Berceo's is a logical
dramatic supposition that the abbot would be suspicious of such a

reminder and that he would investigate and is more likely in an age that savored allegory and implication. Consider quatrain 512:

> Entendió el obispo   enna mesagería
> o qe avién contienda   o fizieron follía
> vino fer su officcio,   visitar la mongía
> ovo a entender   toda la pletesía.

Berceo arouses his audience's more prurient interests as he describes how the abbess is stripped for the clinical examination of the abbot's representatives, none of which is in the Latin version. Then to make the plot even more graphic and lend it a certain logicality, he adds his own personal supposition in 574:

> Metió paz el obispo   enna congregación
> amató la contienda   e la dissensïón,
> quand quiso despedirse,   diólis su bendición
> fo bona pora todos   essa visitación.

Lastly, there is the matter of organization of the materials of plotting. Berceo found reason to alter the structure of the Latin considerably in more than one of the miracles. Dutton traces this very well in his *Comentario* (pp. 157-58) on the Latin and Bercean versions of Miracle XIX, *La preñada salvada por la Virgen,* as well as in Miracle XXI, *La abadesa preñada* (p. 176).

In the realm of plot, then, Berceo, even as he followed his sources, injected his own personal ideas, and these fall well within the realm of originality and creativity. Setting is more elusive than plot in Berceo. But closer inspection proves that he was perfectly conscious of the background the Latin author gave the miracles and realized that it was faulty and colorless. Berceo accepted the geographical locales mentioned in the Latin in nearly every case. For example, as compared with the Latin of the first miracle, which gives the locale in Toledo in a few matter-of-fact words, Berceo amplifies and eulogizes the city, embroidering the Latin "Fuit in toletana urbe" (Dutton, p. 51) in quatrain 1a-b:

> En España cobdicio   de luego empezar,
> en Toledo la magna,   un famado logar,

and with these in the second quatrain a and b:

> En Toledo la buena,   essa villa real,
> qe yaze sobre Tajo,   essa agua cabdal,

both typical amplifications made for the sake of effect, perhaps for authenticity, and to show the poet's pride in Toledo. In Miracle XII Berceo named a foreign city and located it geographically:

> En una villa bona   qe la claman Pavía,
> cibdat de grand facienda,   yaze en Lombardía.
> (281a-b)

Other examples are to be found in XVI, 1a-b, and again in XV, 1a-b, and more could be cited. But geographical settings, even when they demonstrate considerable amplification as to detail and description, are not the most skillful of varieties and do not reveal Berceo's artistic techniques of setting the scenes of the miracles. Sometimes he diminished the setting given him by the Latin but always, it seems, for a definite purpose, for instance, to avoid confusing his audience with names too little known or too exotic.

It is in more indirect ways that his skill in creating artistic settings is evident. A fine example of his studiously undeliberate approach can be found in Miracle XVI, *El judiezno*. The background of the miracle unfolds in a school, a church, and a Jewish home. Berceo's readers or hearers were familiar with schools and certainly they all spent hours in church. The Latin, as it tersely tells its story, mentions that a Jewish boy was instructed along with Christian boys—"qui cum eis litteris instruebatur" (Dutton, p. 129), and the audience had to infer that he went with them to school and then accompanied them to church, "inter illos ad altare accessit et corpus dominicum . . . percepit" (Dutton, p. 129). Berceo embellished this succinct account into a vivid and living setting:

> Tenié en essa villa,   ca era menester,
> un clérigo escuela   de cantar a leer;
> tenié muchos crïados   a letras aprender,
> fijos de bonos omnes   qe qerién más valer.
>
> Venié un judiezno,   natural del logar,
> por savor de los ninnos,   por con ellos jogar;

> acogiénlo los otros,   no li fazién pesar,
> avién con elli todos   savor de deportar.
>
> (354-55)

How much more alive is the scene: the school was needed, it was run by a cleric, and boys were taught to read and sing; there were a great many pupils who were the sons of substantial men; the young Jew was a native of the town and he went to school with them because he liked them and they liked him and did not persecute him (a revealing phrase in itself, for it shows that children were not racists even if their parents were), and that they liked to play with him. By the end of these two quatrains the stage is set and the audience feels at home with the school and with the pupils.

The Latin account merely said that, with the celebrant unawares, the Jewish boy took the wafer. But Berceo, as he characterizes the Jewish child, at the same time sets the scene in the church and enables the audience to "feel" the setting. On Easter Sunday when the Christians went to receive the sacrament, the Jewish child went along with them and wanted to take it, too. His innocence is touchingly revealed in Berceo's quatrain 356c-d.

> príso'l al judïezno   de comulgar grand gana,
> comulgó con los otros   el cordero sin lana.
>
> (356c-d)

The miracle in Latin is a pale sketch of the full-blown account Berceo provides. He relates that they all took the sacrament in great haste, leaving the audience to wonder at first and then to smile at the vision of a harried priest doing all he could to give a group of adolescent boys the sacrament as quickly as possible. And Berceo does not let the opportunity escape him to show the beauty of the Virgin's image and the fact that she holds the Christ Child in her arms:

> Mientre qe comulgavan   a muy gran presura
> el ninno judïezno   alzo la catadura,
> vió sobre'l altar   a una bella figura,
> una fermosa duenna   con genta creatura.
>
> (357)

The image, as seen through the boy's eyes, is effective, for it offers a momentary change of viewpoint and is an unexpected technique on the part of the poet.

Berceo, even as the story moves to its terrible climax filled with details that might claim an audience's entire attention, does not fail to maintain the setting which he employs to create the effect he sought. Whereas the Latin merely said that when the boy got home his father questioned him and, on learning that he had received the Christian sacrament, went wild with rage and cast the lad into a blazing furnace (Dutton, p. 129), Berceo takes time to paint a verbal picture of the father, the room, and the terrible punishment. He blackens the character of the Jew with obvious anti-Semiticism, even mentioning his madness and his gestures, probably to the amusement and, at the same time, the disgust of his audience:

> Pesóli esto mucho   al malaventurado,
> como si lo toviesse   muerto o degollado;
> non sabié con grand ira   qé fer el dïablado,
> fazié figuras malas   como demonïado.
>
> (361)

The reader of the Latin version might have wondered how the blazing furnace happened to be available to the father, since this was not an age of central heating. Berceo at least states that the father kindled the fire:

> Avié dentro en casa   esti can traidor
> un forno grand e fiero   qe fazié grand pavor;
> fízolo encender   el locco peccador,
> de guisa qe echava   sovejo grand calor.
>
> (362)

Then Berceo, conscious of the power of mother love, uses it poignantly making his audience hear her *grandes carpellidas* and see how she tears her cheeks with her fingernails:

> Metió la madre vozes   e grandes carpellidas,
> tenié con sus oncejas   las massiellas rompidas,
> ovo muchas de yentes   en un rato venidas,
> ca de tan fiera quesa   estavan estordidas.
>
> (364)

Belatedly the Latin brings in the grieving mother with its "Mater vero pueri nimio dolore constricta eiulando clamare cepit multosque tan christianos quam iudeos en breve agregavit" (Dutton, p. 129).

Berceo seems even to have taken into consideration the psychological state of mind of the child handled as this Jewish boy had been handled, for when he emerges from the fire and is questioned, the poet has him speak as briefly as a child would under similar circumstances.

> Recudiólis el ninno   palavra sennalada:
> "La duenna qe estava   enna siella orada
> con su fijo en brazos   sobre'l altar posada,
> éssa me defendié   qe non sintía nada."
>
> (369)

The Latin had the child actually speak at this juncture, too, but at more length and in words that one would expect to hear in the mouth of an adult in possession of his emotions. "Quoniam illa veneranda domina que super altare stabat et nobis communicantibus particulas dabat mihi auxilium prebuit et omne incendium a me depulit nec eciam odorem ignis me sentire permisit" (Dutton, p. 129). It must have caused Berceo a slight qualm to give up the concept of no odor of smoke reaching the boy, but he made up for this admirably.

In quatrain 370, he adds another facet to his construction of scene with the logical description of the reaction of the people, as well as the fact that they included this miracle in the repertoire of their tales:

> Entendieron qe era   sancta María ésta,
> qe lo defendió ella   de tan fiera tempesta;
> cantaron grandes laudes,   fizieron rica festa,
> metieron est miraclo   entre la otra gesta.

The Latin also failed to use the materials at hand with which to create the sentiments of the people who had seen the child in the furnace. They reacted just as any mob would have. In the Latin they simply put the Jewish father in the furnace and we read "Qui statim ab igne cruciatus in-momento exustus est totus" (Dutton, p. 129), while Berceo enlivens the passage so that the setting strengthens the plot:

> Quanto contarié omne   poccos pipiones,
> en tanto fo tornado   ceniza e corbones,
> non dizién por su alma   salmos nin oraciones,
> mas dizién denosteos   e grandes maldiziones.
>
> (372)

In most of the miracles Berceo provides setting with characteristic indirectness, which always improves upon the Latin.

Conflict, sometimes strong, sometimes weak—though this last is rare—

is ever-present in Berceo's *Milagros*. External forces, divine or infernal, or human or cosmic provide it. The "classical design" demands that conflict be resolved and it is in each story. The miracle known as *La boda de la Virgen,* number XV, can be used effectively to demonstrate Berceo's treatment of the conflict already present in the Latin source. The story tells of a young canon who was a devotee of the Virgin. When his parents died, his relatives insisted that he marry to perpetuate the family. He agreed to do so, but on the way to the ceremony, remorseful, he went into a church and prayed. There the Virgin spoke to him, setting the exact tone of the conflict when she said:

> "Don fol malastrugado,   torpe e enloquido,
> ¿en qé roídos andas?   ¿en qé eres caído?"
> Semejas ervolado,   qe as yervas bevido,
> o qe eres del blago   de sant Martin tannido.
> (340)

And she continued with the warning that he would be worth nothing if he continued with his plans:

> "Si tú a mi quisieres   escuchar e creer,
> de la vida primera   non te qerrás toller,
> a mí non dessarás   por con otra tener;
> si non, avrás la lenna   a cuestas a traer."
> (342)

So, if he gives up his bride, he angers his people and loses his inheritance, and if he fails to be the Virgin's devotee and celibate, he loses her patronage and incurs her wrath and punishment. Conflict could hardly be more clearly defined. Admittedly it was present in the Latin, but it does not, in the Latin, move the audience as much as does Berceo's picturesque rendition.

The world triumphed, and the young man married, as Berceo intensifies the conflict with a passing remark about the sentiments of "the other woman," that is, the young man's earthly bride who has come between him and the heavenly bride:

> Fizieron ricas bodas,   la esposa ganada,
> ca serié lo al fonta   si fuese desde nada;
> era con esti novio   la novia bien pagada,
> mas non entendié ella   do yazié la celada.
> (344)

The climax of the story comes at bedtime, when it will be decided whether or not the groom can possess his earthly bride; this leads straight to the conflict's resolution:

> Quando veno la noch,   la ora qu dormiessen,
> fizieron a los novios   lecho en qe yoguiessen;
> ante qe entre sí   ningún solaz oviessen,
> los brazos de la novia   non tenién qé prissiesen.
> (347)

The denouement then follows. The resolution of the conflict, begun when the groom cannot consummate his marriage, is finished as the groom steals away, and no one understands why he has left or even where he has gone. The Virgin keeps his secret, and from the words themselves one might think that she has spirited him away miraculously. The Latin merely states "clam domum egressus" (Dutton, p. 123), as compared to Berceo's implication that "los brazos de la novia non tenién qé prissiesen" (347d), as though the bride reaches out to embrace him and finds him no longer there.

Berceo allows the audience to see from his own viewpoint the final resolution, that is, the explanation of the groom's disappearance and probable whereabouts:

> Creemos e asmamos   qe esti bien varon
> buscó algún lugar   de grand religïón,
> y sovo escondido   faciendo oración,
> por ond ganó la alma   de Dios buen gualardón.
> (350)

Also a universal solution is added in the final quatrain, a personal solution for every Christian soul:

> Bien devemos creer   qe la Madre gloriosa,
> porqe fizo est omne   esta tamanna cosa,
> no lo oblidarié,   como es pïadosa,
> bien allá lo farié   posar do ella posa.
> (351)

With such an ending no one could wonder what had taken place and no one could forget the miracle's lesson which is, after all, the resolution of the conflict.

Characterization is an element of considerable substance in Berceo who was a skilled artist in this area of narrative technique. As one who followed the so-called classical design, he concentrates, as had the Latin less effectively, upon a single character, or rarely upon two, as in Miracle X, that of *Los dos hermanos.* He senses the changes influenced by circumstances or inner conflicts, just as he did effectively in *La boda de la Virgen.*

Miracle I, *Milagro de la Casulla de San Ildefonso,* enabled Berceo to exercise markedly his skill in characterization. The Latin had simply revealed that the protagonist was an archbishop named Hildefonsus, who was bright with good works, among which were his attentions and devotions to the Virgin (Dutton, p. 50). Berceo gives this cleric facets of character that delineate him personally and with empathy:

> Ovo un arzobispo,   coronado leal,
> qe fue de la Gloriosa   amigo natural
>   (48c-d)

and he continues with his characterization in quatrain 49:

> Diziénli Yldefonso,   dizlo la escriptura,
> pastor qe a su grey   dava buena pastura,
> omne de sancta vida   qe trasco gran cordura,
> qe nos mucho digamos,   so fecho lo mestura.

There is further strengthening in quatrain 50:

> Siempre con la Gloriosa   ovo su atenencia,
> nunqua varón en duenna   metió mayor qerencia;
> en buscarli servicio   metié toda femencia,
> facié en ello seso   e buena providencia.

To Berceo, then, Yldefonso is not simply accomplished in good works, as the Latin described him, but far more. The two quatrains cited are surely pure characterization.

Throughout the poem Berceo enlivens the Latin, stressing the fervor of Yldefonso's love for Our Lady, personalizing him, making the audience see him as a human and warm devotee.

The villain of the miracle, one Siagrio, a canon who was raised to the dead Yldefonso's place, also is given a stronger characterization than is found in the Latin, which dryly states that he wickedly took over the post and insisted on wearing the chasuble which the Virgin had given to Yldefonso (Dutton, p. 50).

Berceo is more personal and one can feel his effort to paint the canon in the blackest hues:

> Alzaron arzobispo   un calonge lozano,
> era muy sovervioso   e de seso liviano;
> quiso eguar al otro,   fue en ello villano,
> por bien non gelo tovo   el pueblo toledano.
>
> (67)

To make him even less sympathetic Berceo puts hateful words in his mouth, which the Latin also did incidentally with its "Sic ego sum homo, sic et hominem fuisse scio predecessorem meum. Quare ergo non vestire eo quo ieduebatur vestimento, cum eodem quo ipse functus est officio fungar presulatus?" (Dutton, p. 50). Berceo wrote, this time more tersely, but with deeper feeling and therefore greater effect:

> Disso unas palavras   de muy grand liviandat:
> "Nunqa fue Illefonsso   de mayor dignidat,
> tan bien so consegrado   como él por verdat,
> todos somos eguales   enna umanidat."
>
> (69)

Not always does Berceo develop character as carefully as in the cases of Yldefonso and Siagrio, or with as much empathy and sympathy or antagonism, but throughout his *Milagros* he inserts phrases and expressions which add touches of characterization far superior to that of his model.

He never loses sight of the theme of each story, for theme in all of them leads toward the moralization and the didactic preachments he insists upon retaining. Since theme is usually, in the classical design of short fiction, directed toward one person's problem, with peripheral universal implications, Berceo never allowed theme to escape him. Each miracle presents such a person, usually one who has sinned or has been virtuous. If he is in the first category, he will be forgiven or punished, depending upon his attitude, or if he is among the virtuous, he will be rewarded. The Virgin is always depicted as caring for her own, saving each soul, if it is contrite, or punishing it, if it is stubborn and wayward. And by implication, as well as by precise statement, she will save us all or punish us in accordance with our own particular actions and attitudes.

Each miracle ends on these notes of exhortation, some of which are seen in the miracles treated above. The exhortation in Miracle I, since this is fresh in the reader's mind, is an excellent example of the expression of the theme.

> Amigos, atal Madre   aguardarla devemos,
> si a ella sirviéremos   nuestra pro buscaremos;
> onrraremos los cuerpos,   las almas salvaremos,
> por pocco de servicio   grand gualardón prendemos.
> (74)

Miracle III, *El clérigo e la flor,* ends thusly:

> Todo omne del mundo   fará grand cortesía
> qui fiziere servicio   a la Virgo María;
> mientre qe fuere vivo   verá plazentería,
> e salvará la alma   al postremero día.
> (115)

The last quatrain of number VI, *El ladron devoto,* drives home the theme and includes the Savior's grace along with His mother's:

> Las mannas de la Madre   con las d'El qe parió
> semejan bien calannas   qui bien las connoció;
> Él por bonos e malos,   por todos descendió
> Ella, si la rogaron,   a todos acorrió.
> (159)

These are sufficient to indicate that theme is preserved.

Style depends upon clarity in the classic design, as well as upon variety in texture from the plain to the ornate and rich. Sometimes it is consciously designed for language effects. In Berceo much of this last is at work. He made an effort to be clear, to use language and phraseology that his neighbors could understand and enjoy, and he said so in the early lines of *San Millán de la Cogolla.* He was fully aware of the value of the precise word, the exact imagery needed to create the desired effect. In the realm of style one can be almost haphazard in a choice of examples, for Berceo literally interlarded his verses with such effects. How better could one portray a sassy imp of Satan than in dialogue like the following, as that imp argues defiantly with the Virgin? The miracle is number II, *El sacristan fornicario.*

De la otra partida   recudió el vozero,
un savidor dïablo,   sotil e muy puntero:
"Madre eres de Fijo,   alcalde derechero,
que no'l plaze la fuerza   nin es end plazentero.
                                                    (90)

And such a simile as the following must have struck a chord in the
reader's mind, for it appeals to the senses of sight, smell, and taste. The
body of the devotee in Miracle III, *El clérigo y la flor,* has been exhumed
after weeks in the tomb:

Trobáronli la lengua   tan fresca e tan sana
qual parece de dentro   la fermosa mazana;
non la tenié más fresca   a la meredïana
quando sedié fablando   en media la quintana.
                                                    (113)

In describing a monk's illness in Miracle IV, *El galardón de la Virgen,*
he wrote:

Enfermó esti clérigo   de muy fuerte manera,
qe li qerién los ojos   essir de la mollera;
tenié qe era toda   complida la carrera,
e qe li venié cerca   la ora postrimera.
                                                    (123)

The folksy term *mollera* for head was deliberate, of course, and homely
and therefore effective.

The poet's style is racy and piquant in conversations. In number IX, *El
clérigo simple,* we read that the cleric, who knew only one Mass, was
hailed before the bishop. That worthy, enraged, spoke harshly to him:

Fo duramente movido   el obispo a sanna,
dicié: "Nunqua de preste   oí atal hazanna."
Disso: "Dicit al fijo   de la mala putanna
qe venga ante mí,   no lo pare por manna.
                                                    (222)

At this the Virgin rushes to the aid of her devotee and matches harshness
for harshness in her verbal attack upon the bishop:

Díxoli brabamientre: "Don obispo lozano,
¿contra mí por qé fust   tan fuert e tan villano?

Yo nunqa te tollí   valía de un grano,
e tú hasme tollido   a mí un capellano.

(229)

The device of the stylist in Miracle XI, *El labrador avaro,* is intriguing in at least two passages, far removed from the Latin. The perfect word used to paint the farmer in derogatory terms is the one Berceo happened upon in the line "Finó el rastrapaia" ("the haypitcher" [273a]), and equally picturesque is the imagery in quatrain 274c-d, when the angels wish to save the soul from the devils and cannot:

quisieron acorrelli,   ganarla por vecina,
mas pora fer tal pasta   menguavalis farina.

Such homely domestic imagery came naturally to Berceo and would have established strong rapport between him and his audience. The entire quatrain 279 in the same miracle is close to the life of the rural folk who enjoyed the *Milagros*:

Vidiéronla los ángeles   seer desamparada,
de piedes e de manos   con sogas bien atada;
sedié como oveja   qe yaze ensarzada,
fueron e adussiéronla   pora su majada.

Style, then, was one of Berceo's fortes and could be the basis for a long and fruitful study.

Point of view is generally confined to the first person, "author omniscient," or to the third person single character (major or minor). Berceo in his *Milagros* is always the narrator, the author omniscient, and indeed, so much is he so, that he from time to time mentions himself or uses the *yo.* But even as he narrates, he allows flashes of impressionism and emotional reactions to involve the audience and permit it to have its own point of view. An example should suffice. In Miracle XX, *El monje beodo,* such flashes are very bright. Through the use of the "pink elephant motif," so common in stories about drunkards, Berceo leads the reader to a point where he can shake off the bonds of author-omniscience and enter the mind of the drunkard himself, seeing with the drunkard his particular hallucinations. He reads how the drunkard staggers to church, "Peroqe en sos piedes non se podie tener" (465a), and smiles as he discovers that "quísoli el dïablo zancajada [a kick in the rear] poner" (465c). And then, suddenly, the "pink elephant motif" is inserted and the poor fellow sees a raging bull (466). Later, in 470 there appears a fierce dog, and in 473 it is a lion.

> En figura de toro   qe es escalentado,
> cavando con los piedes,   el cejo demudado,
> con fiera cornadura,   sannoso e trado,
> paróseli delante   el traïdor provado.
>
> (466)

In passing, it should be pointed out that the hallucination in Berceo has a more Spanish flavor than the description in Latin, although in the Latin the bull is formidable and terrifying. In the Latin the Virgin described as a *puella* who drives off the bull carrying in her hand a *niveam napulam* "small white napkin," whereas in Berceo's rendition she uses the *falda del manto* and reveals that the Spanish poet knew a good deal more about fighting bulls than had the Latin author.

The Virgin's angry words to the devil, who has frightened the monk with hallucinations, shift the point of view to her and let the audience shift its own:

> "Don falso alevoso,   non vos escarmentades,
> mas yo vos daré oy   lo qe vos demandades;
> ante lo compraredes   qe d'aqend vos vayades,
> con quien volvistes guerra   quiero qe lo sepades."
>
> (477)

Mood and tone, which have inevitably been treated in the earlier categories of Berceo's art, need little further treatment. Suffice to say that his mood is always pious, but with a pietistic structure in which are to be found tenderness, righteous indignation, sympathy, awe—in fact, the entire gamut of human emotion, even humor.

It has not been possible here, in the study of Berceo's narrative techniques, to give a detailed study of all the *Milagros*. The ones treated in detail, however, are representative of the others, except for one single miracle yet to be discussed. This particular miracle, number XXV, is different in so many ways from the other twenty-four that it merits a study in some depth. It may even be an original miracle, one that appears nowhere else.

Miracle XXV,[5] known as *La iglesia robada,* in the *Milagros de Nuestra Señora,* diverges greatly from the others and poses problems which scholars have not solved. Apparently Berceo did not include it in the original version of the *Milagros,* but added it later for reasons he never made clear, reasons which in themselves are intriguing and which have evoked much speculation. It is the only one of the twenty-five *Milagros* which Berceo did not take from the Latin collection of miracles which is known to have been the source of the twenty-four he hispanicized in *cuaderna vía.*

As long ago as 1910 Richard Becker published his findings and revealed that a manuscript in the Library of Copenhagen, known as Thott 128, or else a manuscript identical to it, was Berceo's source, rather than several of the well-known repositories of miracles available, such as the *Speculum Historiale,* the *Legenda Aurea,* and the *Miracles de la Sainte Vierge.*[6] Becker made it clear that Berceo's number XXV was not in Thott 128. As recently as 1971 Brian Dutton studied the *Milagros* against the background of the Copenhagen manuscript, transcending Becker's study in details and readings of the texts, but he was unable to do more, with respect to number XXV, than surmise that it was drawn by Berceo from a written source. His supposition, like that of Becker and of Solalinde, is based upon the last two lines of quatrain 743 (907) ("el miráclo nuevo   fuertment lo recabdaron, / con los otros miraclos   en libro lo echaron") and the last half of the last line in 745 (909) ("como diz la cartiella"). But before one can accept this as incontrovertible evidence of a written source, notwithstanding *cartiella* and *libro,* some arguments to the contrary should be explored. Indeed, Solalinde, before he had finished the preliminary essay for his edition of the *Milagros,* was obliged to conclude that Berceo might have used an oral source.

So radically does XXV differ from the other twenty-four miracles—in content, time, setting, tone, narrative technique, and the pattern of presenting miracles—that this particular miracle may well afford us the only opportunity to study an original creation of Gonzalo de Berceo, or at least a creation not based upon a written source which would have confined the poet as he hispanicized and versified the twenty-four Latin miracles. Number XXV may indeed be the "miraclo nuevo" Berceo labeled it.

Any scholar familiar with folk miracles will detect in XXV elements of popular origin, even at the earliest stage of its development, when rough edges are present, when unnecessary, confusing, and unimportant details are included, much of which, had the miracle been rewritten or retold, would have been deleted in the interest of clarity and overall narrative effect. The miracle as Berceo relates it has the ring of a report or an account just as it happened, and not as generations of raconteurs would have altered it with an eye to improvement. The possibility that the poet was present when the events took place, or that he visited the scene of the miracle shortly after it had occurred, or had a verbal report soon after the occurrence is strong. If any of this supposition is true, the originality of the miracle may reveal a great deal about Berceo's storytelling art that cannot be found in his handling and presentation of the known written sources.

Originality is not necessarily concomitant with narrative art, nor is a story excellent simply because it stems from the folk. *Milagro* XXV as a narrative is inferior in structure to many of the other *Milagros*. The reason probably lies in the antiquity of the others, for all these were "old miracles" in that they had been written long before Berceo saw them, had been recast, perhaps again and again, had been culled of the irrelevant, and had been honed to an almost stark simplicity. Moreover, they had been fitted into the pattern characteristic of medieval miracles in which the concern for the didactic, pious message was as great as the artistic presentation. The "old miracles" belonged to the tradition of clerical brief narratives, they were considered literary by those who wrote them, and they were what people expected to hear or read. The pattern they followed was so well established that Berceo could not stray far from it as he composed his "new miracle."

Inferior to the other miracles or not, number XXV reveals innovations on the part of the poet unlike anything he included in the twenty-four he drew from the Latin. One gets the impression that Berceo, though not constrained by the strictures imposed by the plots and presentations of the written Latin miracles, was guided, though in a different way, and even constrained by an oral account which caused some of the divergences. He found that, not bound by the Latin versions, he could permit himself a certain kind of free rein and could pour into the account a great deal of the contemporary scene, much of local customs, and what appear to be personal observations with an eye to realism and fact, but at the same time this very freedom led to digressions which in some ways actually vitiated the cogency of the narrative.

The thirteenth century was an age of miracles and of the gathering and anthologizing of miracles, both in Latin and in the vernaculars. New miracles were actively sought and quickly committed to writing. Alfonso

X, probably while Berceo still lived, was producing the vast repository of Mary miracles he named the *Cantigas de Santa Maria*.[7] The Learned King himself makes it clear that contemporary or "new miracles" greatly interested him and that he actually traveled on occasion to the scenes of miracles and at times even received gifts that were miraculous in origin.[8] Quite probably Alfonso employed people whose duty it was to gather and assemble contemporary miracles, since it is doubtful that he could have taken the time to ferret out the many which are unique in the *Cantigas*.[9] What is more natural, then, than that Berceo would seize upon a miracle someone told him about or which he was lucky enough to have encountered among the rural folk to whom he ministered? If this is the case, if Miracle XXV was plucked by Berceo from the current and constantly evolving miracle lore of thirteenth-century Spain, then its breaking away from the age-old pattern is explained, as well as its suspected adherence to current and nonliterary patterns.

The formula for most miracles is fairly standard. Early in the miracle the author lays the scene and introduces and characterizes the protagonists. The events leading up to the occurrence of the miracle follow a logical sequence. At the end, the virtuous are rewarded, the sinful punished or pardoned in a way that resolves all the elements of the conflict set up at the beginning. Number XXV diverges from this pattern in unusual ways.

Number XXV begins, as do several others by Berceo, with the statement that he would like to relate another miracle which the Virgin accomplished. But the second quatrain seems to set forth concepts unusual to Berceo, if the poet is actually setting forth something hidden, as is possible. It has been suggested that *li* in the second line of this quatrain means "from her," that is, "from the Virgin." *Li* can be so translated, and if it is, then the stanza simply means that one should be warned by the fate of the priest who stole the Virgin's wimple. If indeed this is the meaning of *li*, then quatrain 704 (968) can be eliminated from the several elements used in my argument. My belief is that *li* means "from it," that is, "from the miracle"; if it does, the argument is strengthened. But with or without this quatrain as evidence, the rest of the argument stands. The doubtful quatrain is as follows:

> Bien creo qe qui esti   miráclo oyere,
> no li querrá toller   la toca qe cubriere:

> ni la querrá por fuerça   toller lo que toviere,
> menbrarli deve esto   demientre qe visquiere.
> (704)

If *li* means "from it," that is, "from the miracle," what is it that is hidden? Does Berceo mean that in the miracle there is something to be concealed from the audience—something into which one must not delve forcefully? If so, this is unlike the presentation of most miracles, since usually all that they contain is meant to be clearly understood.

The third quatrain, without the possibility of denial, sets the miracle apart from the norm: the locale and the time are both Berceo's, and only in number XXV is this the case.

> En el tiempo del Rey   de la buena ventura,
> don Ferrando por nomne,   sennor de'Estremadura,
> nieto del rey Alfonso,   cueropo de grand mesura,
> contio esti miraclo   de mui grand apostura.
> (705)

Ferdinand III, grandson of Alfonso VIII, is the king mentioned. He ruled from 1217 to 1252. Most authorities believe that Berceo was born around 1197 and that he died circa 1246, so the events could quite easily have taken place during his lifetime and that of King Ferdinand III.[10] A more recent estimate of his life, however, is 1196-1260. Even if the king died before the miracle occurred, and even though the death date of Berceo is uncertain, none of this changes in any way the fact that Berceo and Ferdinand were contemporaries. So when Berceo writes of Ferdinand as a king "de la buena ventura," even if this phrase means, as some scholars insist, that he was dead, it does not in any way indicate that the poet and the king were not contemporaries.[11] The setting of the miracle was definitely in Berceo's Spain.

In this Spain that Berceo knew so well, stanza 706 (870) reveals that two robbers left León to come to Castile. One was a layman, the other an ordained priest (707a-b). They reached Çohinos, in the Valladolid region of Castile, a village in the diocese of León. Dutton identifies Çohinos as Ceínos de Campos, Valladolid.

> Moviéronse ladrones   de parte de León
> de essa bispalía.   de essa regïón,

vinieron a Castiella   por su gran confusión,
guïólos el dïablo   qu es un mal guïón.

El uno era lego   en duro punto nado,
el otro era clérigo   del bispo ordenado;
llegaron en Çohinos,   guïólos el Peccado,
el qe guïó a Judas   fazer el mal mercado.

(706-7)

In the outskirts of the village stood a church dedicated to Our Lady (708), and near it the cell of an anchoress. The priest-thief from the outset is seen as an extreme sinner with an unusual kind of wickedness. He differs from other clerical sinners in the *Milagros* in that he commits premeditated felony and breaks one of the commandments, which none of the clerical sinners in Berceo's other miracles does. Priests and nuns in the *Milagros* are led into sin by the devil or are caught off guard by lust, or pride, or some other human frailty.[12] Some scholars even level the accusation at Berceo that he allowed himself frequently and quite noticeably to minimize the clerical vices and sins found in the Latin collection he used.[13] In Miracle XXV this is certainly not the case. The priest-thief is all bad. He has broken the eighth commandment, has disgraced his habit, has renounced his vows, or, if he has not actually renounced them, he sins in a more terrible way as a false priest. It is true that Berceo writes that these robbers were led astray by the very devil who led Judas to "fazer el mal mercado," a significant comparison, but even so the poet makes it very plain that theft is the cleric's chosen profession. He has no virtue whatever, and in accordance with the format of miracles, he should receive the worst of punishments.

The thieves, having broken into the cell of the anchoress, look about for valuables and with shovels dig here and there while the nun hides—709 (873). They find little, for the anchoress has nothing except a very valuable piece of cloth. Berceo's only reason for mentioning this cloth would seem to be that the holy woman actually owned it, and he considered it to be a detail in the story. It has no relevance to the account and, in fact, might even have confused the reader or hearer, since later another piece of valuable cloth, one associated with the image of the Virgin, is of great relevance.

After the thieves had gathered up the contents of the anchoress's cell, they turned to the locked church. Berceo skillfully paints their iniquity:

Lo qe fue en la ciella fue todo abarrido,
malament maneado, en un saco metido;
assaz era el lego omne de mal sentido,
mas de peor el clérigo que más avié leído.
(711)

The robbers pry open the door of the church with shovels and ransack it. The details given in 714 enable the poet to invoke outrage in the minds of his audience:

Despoiaron las sabanas que cubrién el altar
libros e vestimentas con que solién cantar:
fue mal desvaratado el precioso lugar,
do solién pecadores al Criador rogar.

Then they look greedily at the image of Our Lady with her Child and see the fine *toca* it wears. The evil cleric, aware of the worth of sacred vestments, strips the headdress from the image—717 (881). It is a fine touch of characterization on Berceo's part to fix upon and develop the sacrilege and thereby make the cleric even more detestable. He who should have respected holy things, given his calling and his training, was the one to commit the profanation rather than the secular robber. He is the only person in the *Milagros,* clerical or lay, who desecrates an image of the Virgin. People familiar with the pattern of miracles would have expected him to be consumed by fire from heaven or suffer some other terrible fate.

The miracle occurs when the stolen *toca* or wimple wraps itself around the priest-thief's hand thus marking him as the culprit who removed it from the image—719 (883). Miraculous, too, is the strange witlessness that befalls both robbers so that they get lost in the church and wander about blindly.

Stanza 886 might suggest that Berceo followed a written source, but there is another supposition. He was well educated, versed in church history and saintly legend. The reference to Theodore and Pope Clemens need not imply that he did more than provide a comparison drawn from his store of knowledge.[14]

Andavan tanteando de rencón en rencón,
como fazié Sinsinnio el celoso varón,
marido de Teôdora, mugier de gran canción,
la qe por Clemens Papa priso religïon.
(722)

The degree of detailed description in stanza 723 is noteworthy and is not common in the Latin miracles, although Berceo in some of the twenty-four he hispanicized often went far beyond the source and offered many details.

Los locos malastrugos,   de Dios desemparados
andavan como beudos,   todos descalavrados,
oras davan de rostros,   oras de los costados,
de ir en romería,   estavan mal guisados.

The depiction of the capture of the thieves and the rough handling they received after the anchoress had summoned help may reflect Berceo's personal witnessing of their capture or of similar arrests, and of the raw and ugly mob reaction to the desecration of a shrine.

Fueron luego venidos   gran turma de peones,
entraron en la *glesia,*   trovaron los ladrones;
manentráronlos luego   como vinién fellones,
darlis grandes feridas   con mui grandes bastones.

Dávanlis grandes palos   e grandes carrelladas,
coces muchas sovejo   e muchas palancadas;
levavan por los cuerpos   tantas de las granadas
qe todas las menudas   lis eran oblidadas.

(725-26)

The robbers were forced to confess (727) and to explain how the Virgin had captured them. We then read of their sentencing (728-29), or at least of the sentence of death imposed upon the secular thief:

sobre'l lego cativo   prisieron mal consejo:
alzáronlo de tierra   con un duro vencejo.

(729c-d)

The passages in quatrains 730-31 might appear to overburden or even to damage the plot's structure, since the story does not need this incident. However, incidents like it were common in miracle lore. Even had Berceo rewritten or improved the miracle, he might well have allowed it to remain.

Un calonge devoto   omne de sancta vida,
qe tenié so amor   en Dios bien encendida,

quando vío la toca   con la mano cosida,
dizié qe tal justicia   nunqua non fue oida.

Quiso el omne bono   de la toca travar,
en vez de la Gloriosa   el su velo besar,
mas al christiano bono   quísolo Dios onrrar,
despegóse la toca   adiesso del pulgar.[15]

After this digression from the mainstream of the plot, Berceo breaks the miracle pattern one would expect him to follow. The priest-thief's fate was not as simple to resolve as the secular thief's. He had to be judged only in his own diocese. For nine whole quatrains—735-42 (899-906) we read of clerical law and wonder why Berceo devoted so much space to it. He did nothing like this in any other miracle, nor did his sources for the other miracles. Was he breaking the pattern of miracle narration because he was reporting all the events surrounding the miracle, even when those events did not contribute to the miracle's plot? The priest-thief, according to the formula of miracle lore, should have been put to death or killed by divine intervention, since he was a far greater sinner than his secular partner. It may be that the entire sequence of the legal rights of the criminal was included by the poet because he actually considered it as part of what happened in the aftermath of the miracle. Had he rewritten the miracle later, I believe that he would have omitted these nine quatrains.[16]

Since the legal sequence may support the argument that Berceo felt that he had to report all the facts surrounding the miracle, some more detailed reference to these passages is needed.

The Leónese bishop of the diocese in which the profanation had taken place came to Çohinos (*Dios lo quiso guiar*) and found that he had to deal with the problem (732a). He therefore took the bad priest to his headquarters in the city of León. Once in the city, the bishop states that he cannot judge the priest, having learned that he is from another diocese, that of Avila.

"Amigos,—diz el bispo,—   esto es aguisado,
non es nuestro el clérigo,   nin de nuestro bispado:
por nos non es derecho   que sea condenado:
júdguelo su obispo,   su mercet, su peccado.

Por del obispo de Avila   se es él aclamado,
clámase por su clérigo   e de su obispado:

judgar ageno clérigo   por leï es vedado,
podría yo por ello   después seer reptado.

(740-41)

The bishop in León sends off the criminal to the bishop in Avila with a threat, one incidentally that he could hardly have carried out, given the rights of priests already discussed. Perhaps the bishop uttered the threat to show his people that he did not condone the crimes the man had committed, and if he did utter them, then Berceo recorded them, again because he had either heard the words or was told what the bishop had said.

Mas pongo tal sentencia   qe se açotado,
qe si trovado fuere   en todo est bispado,
sea luego pendudo,   en un árbol colgado;
el qui lo perdonare   sea descomulgado.

(742)

The last, and one of the most striking, violations of the miracle pattern is the ending of the story. It is what modern fiction writers refer to as a "walk-away ending," for it certainly does not resolve the conflict and leaves the priest-thief's fate a mystery. Such an ending is not to be found elsewhere in Berceo, and he must have so written it because he did not know the fate of the thief and therefore could do no more than offer a surmise about it.

Nunqa más lo veyeron   desqe lo envïaron,
en todo el bispado   nunqa lo testiguaron;
el miráculo nuevo   fuertment lo recabdaron,
con los otros miraclos   en libro lo echaron.

(743)

How convincing, as to a written source, are the last two lines? Who gathered up the new miracle and who put it in a book? In what book? With what other miracles? Could not Berceo be talking about his own book, his *Milagros de Nuestra Señora?* Might not he have preferred to say, "They put it in a book," rather than "I put it in a book?" Or could "they" not have taken the miracle which Berceo versified and have put it in a book? How many scholars today have said "they" published my article in such-and-such a journal?

As to the other reference to written form, "como diz la cartiella," how convincing is it? This reference does not prove that Berceo used a written source, because we do not know to what *cartiella* refers.

> Los malos qe vinieron afontar la tu ciella,
> bien los tovisti presos dentro en tu capiella;
> al bon omne qe quiso vesar la tu toquiella,
> bien suelta gela disti, como diz la cartiella.
>
> (745)

When the poet mentions *cartiella,* he may refer to the miracle he himself wrote. Or *cartiella* need not signify some written source Berceo might have used. The word might even mean, in the way Berceo used it, something like "proverb" or "saying," making quatrain 909 mean "You gave it to him, as the saying (proverb) goes."

Miracle XXV is indeed a "new miracle" and even a roughhewn miracle, as regarded from the technical narrative point of view. It may even be regarded as a kind of poetic "first draft," composed on the very scene of the miracle and at the very time it occurred, or soon thereafter. All that Berceo saw or heard about it he included in the poem. Probably he never rewrote it or polished it. What he produced is a story unhampered by the strictures of a written source, but nonetheless conversely bound by an oral source which in its own different way was also binding, even though it permitted more originality. Its innovations as well as its imperfections in narrative technique and structure may reveal more of Berceo's artistry, excellent or poor, as a raconteur, than anything else he wrote.

Berceo's *Milagros de Nuestra Señora* are, then, his greatest contribution to the genre of brief narrative in verse in medieval Spanish literature. Each is a separate brief narrative, each is handled as an individual unit, and no miracle depends upon another in any way. In the *Milagros* it has been easy to demonstrate the degree to which Berceo followed the hallowed "classic design" of storytelling and to reach the conclusion that his narrative techniques excelled those found in his Latin model. It is not difficult to see, then, why the poet of La Rioja attained a lofty reputation as a poet and a raconteur and why, though often studied, his *Milagros* are still under scrutiny and are the subjects of present-day criticism.

His other works have not been overlooked by scholars, but they have not received the attention they merit as repositories of brief narrative and of the techniques employed to present brief narratives.

BERCEO'S *VIDAS* AND HIS *MARTIRIO*

The lives of three saints versified by Gonzalo de Berceo merit consideration in any investigation of his narrative technique. There were three—
Vida de San Millán de la Cogolla, Vida de Santo Domingo de Silos, and
Vida de Santa Oria.[17] The *passio,* or martyrdom, represented in Berceo's
works by the *Martirio de San Laurençio,* resembles the *Vidas* in a number
of ways.

The *Vida de Santo Domingo de Silos,* a poem of 3,108 verses, or 777
monorhymed quatrains, contains three parts and is the longest of Berceo's
works. Its tripartite division follows the traditional formula of the genre
of the *vita sancti.* Each part is actually a separate unit since each has a
beginning, a sustained argument, and a definite denouement. Each is,
therefore, a brief narrative. The *vida,* viewed as a whole, may also be
regarded as a longer brief narrative. After all, if one deletes the many interpolated miracles, its frame story is not as long as *Santa Maria Egipciaca,* which has been treated earlier as a brief narrative. In barest outline
this typical *vita sancti* devotes its first division to the childhood and early
manhood of the protagonist; the second to the miracles wrought by him in
later life; and the third narrates the miracles performed after his death.
Such is the pattern of this Spanish *vida* and, for that matter, of most *vidas*
in Spanish and in other medieval languages.

Berceo, obviously motivated by great devotion to Santo Domingo, who
died in 1073, wrote with sympathy and empathy and made a considerable
effort to establish rapport with his audience. He uses most of the techniques he employed in his miracles of the Virgin, that is, popular
language, direct address, the first person, homely vocabulary, colloquial
diminutive endings, and, in general, the syntax and figures of speech
familiar to his readers or to those who heard his works read aloud.
Likewise, he followed the "classic design" and did not forget to reckon
with conflict, characterization, setting, point of view, theme, and mood or
tone. How much more successful must have been his poetic rendition than
Grimaldus's Latin prose, for it was the monk Grimaldus who in the
eleventh century wrote the original Latin version.

In the second quatrain Berceo also seeks affinity with his public,
pleading ignorance and stressing his desire to make himself understood in
the local vernacular, all of which argues for a popular audience, not an
erudite one:

> Quiero fer una prosa   en roman paladino,
> En qual suele el pueblo   fablar a su veçino,
> Ca non so tan letrado   por fer otro latino,
> Bien valdrá, commo creo,   un vaso de bon vino.
> (2)

Surely no poet's efforts to attract his audience could be more pronounced. He cannot read Latin well, he states (this was not true, by the way), leading his hearer or reader to identify more readily with a poet who was regarded as a simple man; he uses *roman paladino,* "plain Spanish," the language all could follow; and likening himself to the troubadours and *juglares* of secular narrative poetry, he stated that his efforts will be worth a glass of good wine.

With affinity between author and audience established, Berceo pens the first division which is easily seen to follow the model of other *vitae sanctorum,* a stricture that Berceo cannot avoid because he was constrained to use the material in the Latin prose account of the life of Santo Domingo by Grimaldus. We read therefore of the model child as he grew up in Cañas, of his youthful days as a shepherd, of his rare facility at learning, of his life as a hermit, and later, as when he fled the jealousy of his fellow monks in the monastery of San Millán de la Cogolla, Berceo's own favorite religious establishment.

Toward the end of the first division, Berceo again seeks affinity with the public, in a discussion of Domingo's efforts to restore to its pristine glory the ruined monastery of Santa María at Cañas, efforts at rapport that cannot be overemphasized. He went so far as to include in the *vida* elements from his own personal life:

> Yo Gonzalo, que fago   esto a su amor,
> Yo la vi, assi veya   la faz del Criador,
> Una chica coçina   asaz poca labor,
> Y escriben que la fizo   esse buen confessor
> (109)

The first division also treats historical persons. In a sequence of events, itself a well-rounded brief narrative, the poet writes of Domingo's defiance of King García of Nájera, because the king demanded great sums from the monastery treasury. Related also are the saint's refusal to live in this king's realm and Domingo's flight to Castile, where Ferdinand I of

Castile and León ruled, whose assistance enables Domingo to rebuild the old monastery of Silos of which he is made abbot.

The second division, also in full accord with the tenets of the pan-European *vita sancti,* relates the thirteen miracles Santo Domingo performed while he governed the monastic community at Silos. The saint heals people of paralysis, blindness, withered limbs, twisted bodies, gout, leprosy, and lameness; more interesting miracles are those in which he faces diabolical possession or when he outwits dishonest beggars and overcomes robbers who attempt to sack the monasteries. Of note, also, is Domingo's success in accomplishing the escape of captives held in Moorish dungeons. Each miracle is narrated with the empathy found in the *Milagros de Nuestra Señora.* Some run for only a few lines, while others are as long as the shorter miracles of the Virgin.

The last division of the *vida* presents twenty-two miracles wrought by the saint after he had gone to heaven. Most of these take place at the saint's tomb to which the lame, the halt, the blind, and the possessed have been brought.

The *Vida de San Millán de la Cogolla,* composed of 489 quatrains, that is 1,956 verses, may be regarded as more catholic in the variety and quality of the twenty-six miracles it contains. The first division, in the traditional development of the genre of the *vita sancti,* is a succinct brief narrative in itself and resembles the *Vida de Santo Domingo.* The child Millán lives as a shepherd until God influences him in a vision to seek religious education. Once he has received this training, he goes into the wilderness of Cogolla, defeats dangerous beasts, and is a hermit until his fame attracts pilgrims whose attentions drive him deeper into the wilderness. Vivid is the poet's description of his actions:

> Ovose de las cuevas   por esso a mover,
> De guisa nol podió   nul omne entender:
> Metiose por los montes   por mas se esconder,
> Con les bestias monteses   su vida mantener
> (47)

But at last he returns to civilization, is ordained, and goes back to the village of Berceo to become a secular priest. Envious and hateful monks lead him to a second flight to the wilderness. Part II relates a series of nineteen miracles: the saint cures the blind, the dying, the man whose belly is swollen with humors; he restores withered hands and exorcises devils.

More novel is the way the saint turned water into wine for a feast, made a wooden beam lengthen so as to fit the church for which it was intended, and gave the lie to the devil who had publicly accused him of fornication with pious women. After Millán died and had gone to heaven, his tomb became the site of miracles.

In Part III, the dead Saint Millán cures the blind, sends heavenly oil to replenish a sacred lamp about to flicker out, and resuscitates a dead girl. In this section there is a short history of the Moorish invasion and the enslavement of Spain, replete with the motif of tribute in the form of maidens. No less heroes than Fernán González and King Ramiro, who are aided by the direct intervention of Saint James and Saint Millán, play a role in this third section.

Each division is a brief narrative in itself, just as each miracle is also a brief narrative; so is the sequence about the Moorish invasion. Indeed, the entire *vida* is a somewhat lengthy brief narrative.

In the case of the *Vida de San Millán de la Cogolla,* Berceo has drawn upon a Latin source, the *Vita Sancti Aemiliani* of the sixth century written by Saint Braulius. Out of that terse prose account, he composed a masterpiece in his own vernacular.

The *Vida de Santa Oria,* shortest of Berceo's *vidas,* since it contains only 205 quatrains, was written when he was old, as he himself tells us:

> Quiero en mi vegez,   maguer so ya cansado,
> De esta sancta Virgen   romanzar su dictado.
> (5-6)

This third and last saint's life is not a bouquet of miracles like the lives of the two male saints: it is instead rather a single narrative which relates the life and suffering, as well as the visions and entry into heaven, of the virgin Oria. A softer and more tender tone of deep reverence for the pious Oria and a unique mystic quality differentiate it from the other two *vidas.* The structure of this interesting *vida,* as T. A. Perry points out, is tripartite, like Berceo's other two *vidas.* [18] The first division, made up of the first twenty-four quatrains, narrates Oria's childhood and adolescence; the second division, quatrains 25-184, describes her visions, substituting these for the miracles in other *vidas;* and the third division, quatrains 190-205, describes a vision inspired by the saint after her death.

Perry points out that the poet structures this poem in a way superior to the development of *San Millán* and *Santo Domingo.* Whereas in those *vidas* he presented the series of miracles, one after another, without variation, he avoids this monotony in the *vida* of Oria. All the visions are arranged skillfully in diminishing biographical importance and of ascending spiritual importance. Oria's death offers still another structural improvement, one which does not occur in between two series of miracles. Oria's death is predicted in the second vision and partly revealed in the vision of the Mount of Olives. Then, death comes and the didactic end is fulfilled, rounding out remarkably the thematic and structural development of the poem's second part. The plot in brief is this. Oria was holy, even as a child. As a young girl, she fasted and mortified the flesh so rigorously that she could hardly move about. One night she experiences a vision. Saints Agatha, Eulalia, and Cecilia appear to her and praise her highly. Their words are warm and filled with sentiment. People who read or heard what these saints said would have been moved:

> Combidarte venimos,   nuestra hermana,
> Embianos don Christo,   de quien todo bien mana,
> Que subas a los çielos,   e que veas que gana
> El serviçio que faces   e la saya de lana.
>
> (33)

In this vision Oria goes with the saints to heaven, and, as guides, they explain much about the angelic beings she sees there—saints, virgins, martyrs. Ingenuously, in quatrain 80, one reads of her glimpse of the Apostles:

> Vido a los apostolos   mas en alto logar,
> Cada uno en su trono   en que debia jusgar
> A los evangelistas   y los vido estar,
> La su claridat omne   non la podrie contar.
>
> (86)

She sees a throne and learns that it is to be her own. She would prefer to stay in heaven, but God Himself tells her she must return to earth to live out her life. The words put into the mouth of God the Father as he comforts Oria and tells her to have faith that she will be with Him in heaven are:

> "Lo que tu tanto temes   e estás desmedrida,
> Que los çielos son altos,   enfiesta la subida,

Io te los faré llanos,   la mi fixa querida,
Que non havrás embargo   en toda tu venida.''

                                (106)

Oria returns, later to be visited by the Virgin herself, who presents her with a wondrously beautiful and comfortable bed, promising her that very soon she will be in heaven. Soon thereafter Oria goes to heaven, to appear in a vision to Amuna, her mother, to tell her of her own place there. The mother questions her daughter and inquires about her companions in heaven. Oria replies:

"Entre los inoçentes   so, madre heredada,
Los que puso Erodes   por Christo a espada,
Yo non lo merezria   de seer tan honrrada.
Mas plogó a don Christo   la su virtut sagrada.''

                                (200)

The poem ends with Oria returning to heaven, after leaving Amuna.

Berceo's source was a Latin prose *vita* written by the maiden Oria's confessor, a certain Munno (in Latin Munnius), as is made clear in quatrain 5:

Munno era su nonbre,   omne fue bien letrado,
Sopo bien su façienda,   el fizo el dictado.

Munno wrote the *vita* probably after Oria's death in 1069, and no one else, it is believed, wrote about her life and visions until Berceo came upon Munno's text which he so lovingly versified. Her life would not be set down again until Padre Prudencio de Sandoval rendered it into prose and saw it published in 1601.

The three *vidas,* then, in general illustrate Berceo's narrative techniques as they have been described more fully as to the *Milagros de Nuestra Señora.* The fact that the *Milagros* were adapted from a Latin collection which was current in Spain as elsewhere and that the three *vidas* stemmed from saints' lives written in Latin about Spaniards and by Spaniards does not seem to alter the Bercean approach.

Berceo's *El martyrio de San Laurençio* is also a brief narrative in verse, but shows substantial differences from his other saints' lives. Berceo knew this, of course, and made it clear to his audience from the outset that he had written something apart from his three *vidas.* In the first quatrain he wrote, "Quiero fer la passion de sennor Sant Laurent.'' The work, then, is not simply a *vida:* it is a *passion,* and a *passion* is seen to be a blend of *vita sancti* and *passio,* which is not rare in Latin and in vernacular writings.

Elements of originality in this earliest extant Spanish account of Saint Laurence's martyrdom can be seen in the techniques the poet used. The brief 105 verses, like all his other poems, are couched in the monorhymed quatrains of the *mester de clerecía,* and his custom of interpolating gems of quaint dialogue, colloquial issues, characteristic diminutive endings, folksy expressions, and idiomatic constructions and syntax common to his native region is exercised fully. As usual, the poem is in the first person and the poet speaks directly to his audience, calling his hearers *amigos* and using the pronoun *vos.*

Less visible, but present nevertheless, is a tripartite structure—the youth of Laurençio and early service in Spain; his manhood at the papal court with the emperor's persecution of the faithful; and finally the trial and torment of the saint.

The argument of the *passion* is simple, and all references to the protagonist's childhood are omitted. One reads only that Laurençio was a young and well-educated cleric in the service of Bishop Valerio of Huesca. His character is so fine that he is allowed to accompany his superior to the papal court. Pope Sixtus quickly sees his virtues and demands the young priest's services. So it is that in His Holiness's household, Laurençio rises to prominence and is noted for good works. When the Emperor Decius cruelly persecutes his Christian subjects—among these Laurençio—and gives him the choice of sacrificing to the Immortal Gods or be executed and also handing over to Decius the church treasury, Laurençio instead gives the money to the poor. When asked to produce it, he presents the poor people themselves, calling them the treasure. The lines are stirring.

> Estos son los tesoros   que nunqua evegeçen,
> Quanto mas se derramen,   siempre ellos mas creçen,
> Los que a estos aman   e a esto offreçen,
> Essos avran el reyno   do las almas guareçen.
>
> (97)

The furious emperor offers Laurençio one final opportunity to adore the gods and produce the treasure, but Laurençio defies him:

> Dissoli Sant Laurençio: todas tus amenazas
> Mas sabrosa me saben   que unas espinazas,

> Todas los tus privados,   nin tu que me porfazas,
> Non me fechas mas miedo   que palomas torcazas
> (87)

In the course of this *passio,* only two miracles emerge, in both of which blindness is cured, and each account is so brief that it barely fulfills the qualifications of brief narrative.

As in all the versions of Saint Laurence's martyrdom, in Latin and in the vernaculars, the poet focuses upon the terrible tortures the saint endures as he dies upon the grill. The Spanish poet's direct source was probably the account of the martyrdom written by Saint Ambrose himself rather than a version of Ambrose rewritten by some other poet, for example, Prudentius, who treated this martyrdom in his *Peristephanon* (ca. 400). The events—indeed, even the very dialogues found in Ambrose—appear along with the same macabre humor described by Curtius and Delehaye. Laurençio speaks to his tormentors:

> Pensat, diz Laurençio,   tornar del otro lado,
> Buscat buena pevrada,   ca azaz so assado,
> Pensat de almorzar,   ca avredes lazdrado
> Fijos, Dios vos perdone   da feches grant pecado!
> (104)

In this *vita-passio,* of which some final verses are missing, Berceo is less facile and charming than usual. The interpolated miracles are not as well developed, and the entire piece is simply inferior to his three longer *vidas.* It can be surmised that the genre of the *passio* was not as familiar to Berceo, or not as well liked by him as was the *vita sancti.*

Berceo's shorter poems cannot be regarded as brief narratives or repositories of brief narratives. It is true that the *Duelo que fizo la Virgen Maria el Dia de la Pasion de su Fijo Jesu Christo* contains narrative passages, since it treats the events surrounding the Crucifixion, paraphrasing biblical passages, employing dialogue and Bercean imagery and other narrative techniques so dear to the poet; even so, the events are essentially those recounted in Holy Scripture and have therefore not been included in this investigation of Berceo's narrative techniques. The same may be said in the case of brief narrative passages in the *Loores de Nuestra Señora* and the long *De los signos que aparesceran antes del Juicio.* Each of these narrates happenings and to this extent they are brief narratives, but they do not fall within the purview of the present study.

LA VIDA DE SAN ILDEFONSO

It would be peculiar, in a land as large as Spain and as heavily populated as it was in Berceo's time, if other saints' lives had not been written. Of course others were, but so far these have not measured up to Berceo's. A poet, probably later than Berceo, composed a *Vida de San Ildefonso* (Berceo's first *milagro* in the *Milagros de Santa Maria* was about the same person), but as compared to the Bercean version it is a poor thing indeed. Its *cuaderna vía* is by no means as artistic and poetic as Berceo's, for it sometimes far exceeds the fourteen-syllable count and sometimes diminishes that number of syllables to as few as ten; on occasion it even fails to progress in monorhymed quatrains, although generally the poet made an effort to do so. And yet, the poem has a rude charm, with occasional flashes of brilliance. Like Berceo the poet followed the tradition of the *vita sancti,* dividing his work into the usual three parts; conflict is established in each part and resolved at its end; attention is given to plot, less to setting; certainly there is considerable in the realm of characterization; theme is the usual, and effect is single in purpose. The point of view is omniscient, and the mood or tone runs all the way from the serious to the lightly comic or satiric.

The childhood of the saint is especially well handled, with age-old motifs found in all accounts of the lives of holy men. His mother prays to the Virgin for a son and in a vision, the Virgin visits her and promises her one. The poet slips in the lesson that any woman in trouble can have aid from Our Lady. His mother dedicated his life to the Virgin, and by the time the child Alfonso (in the poem Ildefonso is called Alfonso) is two years old, he can sing the *Ave Maria.* When is he old enough to read he is taken to Saint Eugenio who finds him the best student he has ever taught. He is described as so scholarly that he surprised people:

> E marabillados eran de como aprendia
> Que a grandes e a chicos a todos los vençia
> (72-73)

He is made to seem very saintly at a tender age and is already too holy to be a normal child:

> Ibanse con él de ninnos una grand companna;
> Si habia en si alguno alguna mala manna

Castigavale Alfonso con alguna buena fasanna
E tolliele las costumbres porque se el alma danna.
(78-81)

Part I of the three-part *vida* is taken up, then, with the pious childhood and young manhood of Ildefonso. He leaves his region and goes to Seville to study with Saint Isidore, and once he is educated to his own and the saint's satisfaction, he asks permission to go home. Some conflict develops here, since Isidore feels that he cannot dispense with the help of such a paragon. But at length permission is granted and the young priest returns to Toledo. The poet narrates entertainingly the events surrounding his arrival with touches of sentiment that must have been pleasing to all who heard or read them.

El bendicho criado fuele luego las manos besar,
Alli comenzaron amos muy fuerte a llorar.
Con grand alegria non pudo fablar.
En pos del arzobispo fue su padre llegando,
Omillóse el fijo e las manos le besando,
Tornó a la çuidat reyendo e jugando.
(196-201)

Then an even greater conflict comes: Ildefonso's mother and his uncle want him to rise in the hierarchy, but instead he enters a poor monastery and shuns honors, which makes his father grow violent in his efforts to restrain him. The father's character is developed realistically: he has spent his substance on the son's education and now the young man will throw it away. Ildefonso tries to avoid the older man, but is found in the monastery in his habit. The father, a powerful man, goes to the archbishop:

E dixo, sennor, grand cuita vos vengo a desir
Como el abat Dios dado vos sopo deservir,
Sopo al arçidiano malamente escarnir
E a mi a su madre matar e destruir.
(257-60)

But the archbishop mollifies the father, Ildefonso's mother who hoped that her son would take holy orders is delighted, and the action, having reached a climax, ends on a peaceful note. While there is no visible break in the poem, nor any sign that a sequence has ended, one has, and what has taken place can be considered as a complete narration.

E don maestre Alfonso fincó asosegado
En serviçio de Dios poniendo su cuidado,
De la Virgen preçiosa siervo tan acabado,
Que todos le llamaban el bienaventurado.
(465-68)

Part II reveals that Ildefonso succeeded so well in the monastery that the brotherhood wanted to make him abbot, but he wishes no honor; still, when the archbishop of Toledo dies, he is made archbishop. As a devotee of the Virgin he writes a book in her honor and renews her veneration in all Spain. She speaks to him and promises great esteem. It is at this juncture that the poet inserts a sermon which Ildefonso preached and an explanation by him of the Annunciation and the birth of the Savior, all of which the clergy knew perfectly well. Then he asks for a special feast day for Our Lady, but nothing is said, as was the case in Berceo's miracle, about moving the day from March to December.

Here, in the midst of the honors done the Virgin by Ildefonso, are inserted miracles. Saint Leocadia comes out of her tomb to greet Ildefonso. Almost immediately comes another: the Virgin, surrounded by angels and a choir of virgins, promises him a place beside her in heaven; then she gives him the heavenly chasuble, making plain the taboo connected with it, for no one else must ever wear it.

The second part of the poem draws to a close, completing what can be regarded as a complete brief narrative. Toledo is glorified due to the Virgin's gratitude to the city, the people are content, and Ildefonso is their famous bishop:

La Reyna Madre de santa piadat,
Bendixo a don Alfonso, por cuya santidat
Es oy ensalzada Toledo la çibdat.
Toda la gente andaba ende mas muy gososa,
Mostrando que tenie la voluntat pagada,
Para servir a vos e a la Gloriosa,
Que les asi honraron de tan noble cosa.
(886-95)

The third and last sequence, beginning with line 894, a complete narrative in itself, relates that Ildefonso lived a long time until God called him. Led by angels he departs, leaving the city of Toledo in mourning. The reader is made to see death in his case as a beautiful thing:

Quano el cuerpo llevaban, non semejaba muerto,
Tan blanco iba como la nieve del puerto.

The body remained intact and the sick who came near it were cured. The new conflict builds up right after the burial, for a new prelate had to be elected. It will be recalled that in Berceo the new archbishop was Siagrio. Later Alfonso X in his *Cantigas de Santa Maria* would perpetuate the name in his rendition in Galician-Portuguese. But the unknown poet of the *Vida de San Ildefonso* uses a different name calculated to arouse rancor against the hateful man. One wonders if it did not also make his audience smile:

Escogieron a uno, en fuerte punto fue nado.
Este fue Detestado, su nombre era tal.
(936-37)

All were pleased with Detestado at first, but soon he began to reveal his true colors:

Despues que se vió el loco arzobispo alzado,
Tomó muy gran soberia el mal aventurado,
Porque lo hobo de Dios asi desamparado,
Que le fuera mejor morir en otro estado.
(941-44)

Suspense builds from the moment the audience realizes that Detestado plans to wear the sacred chasuble. Everyone warned him not to anger the Blessed Virgin. But, using the word *nos* to vaunt his new estate of importance, he insisted and even went so far as to belittle the dead Ildefonso:

Dixo él, nos non la habemos de vestir liçençia,
Luego vayan por ella sin otra detenençia.
Como era perlado el nuestro anteçesor,
Bien asi somos nos perlado e pastor,
Como nos escogiestes por nos faser menor.
(955-59)

The treasurer had to go for the chasuble. And the poet remarks to the audience, with reference to the new bishop:

E fuera muy mejor que non fuese levantado.

In Berceo's version (quatrain 72), when the taboo was broken, Siagrio was strangled by the vestment, but the poet of the *Vida* waxes more graphic and ferocious as he describes the scene. Nearly everyone must have known the famous miracle, and some who heard or read the version in the *Vida* must have known the Bercean rendition, as well as the Alfonsine. And yet new details appear, perhaps included to shock:

Asi como primero probo por la vestir,
Non lo quiso la Virgen nin Christo consentir,
Ca hobo él so ella mala muerte a morir,
Una muerte tan fea que non querria desir.
Echando sobre sí la santa vestidura,
Así lo apretó al ome sin ventura,
Que lo fiso partir por medio de la çintura,
Onde non pesó a muchos, nin havian ende cura.
(963-70)

The poem ends in a sermonlike way, driving home the reason for the death of Detestado and making it clear that Ildefonso did much to make Toledo the most famous city of Spain, as did other bishops like Eugenio and Juliano. There is the usual exhortation to Jesus and God to preserve us all from sin and danger, none of which has to do with the events surrounding the life of Ildefonso.

In essence *La vida de San Ildefonso,* even today, is worth reading. Though its poetic structure is irregular and often faulty, it follows the classic design. Each of its three divisions develops conflict and reaches a climax; setting is made a definite part of the story, for Toledo, Spain's "holy city," is ever present as background and most definitely affects the story itself; characterization for the protagonist and the antagonist is well handled, given the models the poet followed and the audience he wrote to impress; the theme revolves around Ildefonso's piety and Detestado's wickedness; style is strong enough to catch and hold attention, although certain digressions, principally in the form of pious remarks and sermonlike sequences, mar it; there are really two effects—the first, the exemplary devotion of Ildefonso to Our Lady and its reward in the form of a heavenly garment to honor him in this life and a place in heaven after his death; the second, the blasphemy of the haughty new archbishop and divine retribution. Point of view, which is omniscient, never fluctuates, leaving the audience with a feeling of security in the face of facts and a plot related by one familiar with the story. The mood or tone is two-pronged: a warm rapport is quickly developed in the audience for Ildefonso from his birth until his death and ascension into heaven; and an instant dislike, which soon turns into active hate, for the vain and overweening Detestado. Even when his body lay cut in two by the chasuble, the sight grieved few, nor did people mind what had happened to him.

Little is known about the author. He reveals the paucity of extant information:

> E el de la Magdalena hobo en ante rimado,
> Al tiempo que de Ubeda era benefiçiado.
> Despues quano esto fiso, vivia en otro estado.
> (1016-18)

Obviously he was a churchman, perhaps he was the author of a lost life of the Magdalene. Whoever he was, he had a deep sense of dedication and devotion to the Toledan hierarchy of bishops and for San Ildefonso in particular, for he wrote with feeling and with considerable poetic skill, although this flags from time to time.

Chapter Four

The *Cantigas de Santa Maria* of Alfonso X el Sabio

Brief narrative in verse continued beyond the days of Berceo. Indeed, during Berceo's last years—if he died around 1246, as is generally believed—a new troubadour of the Virgin was already beginning the most extensive and artistic repository of sacred brief narratives in the Middle Ages. He is, of course, Alfonso X el Sabio, who began his rule in 1252 and died in 1284.[1] Born in 1221, he spent an active youth and learned much about life at court, in the army, and as a scholar. The best teachers were his— musicians, legists, theologians, rhetoricians, and historians. At his mother's knee he must have heard many family legends, as well as pious tales and miracles, and his instruction by the clergy, which of necessity was extensive, would have familiarized him with many more. Still another part of a many-faceted upbringing were those years of his youth spent under the tutelage of an *ayo* or tutor-guide, a nobleman named Don Garci Fernández and of his wife Doña Mayor Arias. Like other princes' and nobles' sons he was sent to live far from court and parents in the rural atmosphere of Galicia where Don Garci's ancestral holdings lay.[2] Galicia was the home of the troubadours, many of whom would have visited the home of Alfonso's *ayo,* and it was from these musicians that the young Alfonso must have gained his training in the soft, sweet brand of the Galician tongue so loved and used by lyric poets both in Portugal and in Spain.

In Galicia, too, he learned a more earthy variety of Galician, for he was brought up with the children of the district, the sons and daughters of the nobility as well as with the children of their servitors. Surely these critical years in the boy's life spent in a land famous for its legends and superstitions left a permanent mark upon Alfonso. He never forgot Galicia, nor did he forget Don Garci and Doña Mayor, for he made bequests to them in his will.

The influence of his father, Fernando III el Santo, was still another factor in his life. Devoted to his sire who would be sainted for his support of the Christian faith against Islam, he emulated him in many ways. From his father, quite probably, he inherited his devotion to the Virgin as an ally in warfare and from his mother, Queen Beatriz, his conception of Our Lady as the advocate of the weak, the needy, and the troubled.

Whether or not Alfonso had begun to collect and write miracles of the Virgin before his coronation cannot be ascertained. It is believed that the first 100 of the *Cantigas* had been completed by 1257, only five years after he was crowned. But given his great enthusiasm for miracle lore, it is possible that his interest developed early, as has been suggested, perhaps even in his childhood. He may even have read Berceo's *Milagros,* for it is known that he visited the Monastery of Santo Domingo at Silos in 1255, some nine or ten years after the death of Berceo. Alfonso was thirty-four years old at the time. It is possible, then, that he had read some of Berceo's works. It is even likely, for that matter, that he had visited that monastery earlier, as well as the Monastery of San Millán de la Cogolla, even while Berceo still lived. A meeting between the two devotees of the Virgin makes delightful speculation. By the time of such a meeting, Berceo would have composed his *Milagros* and might well have become, because of those poems, as well as because of his *Vidas,* a local celebrity. The *Cantigas* themselves reveal that Alfonso actually traveled to shrines at which miracles had taken place.[3] Most probably he visited these places to verify the authenticity of the miracles, to study their background, or to savor the pious atmosphere where divine intervention had actually manifested itself.[4] There was, then, considerable opportunity for the erudite prince to have visited the rural poet, and reasons for such a visit are varied and feasible.

Whether Berceo's *Milagros* influenced Alfonso's may never be known with surety, even though some of the miracles related by Berceo are found in the *Cantigas.* But that the genre of pietistic writing which the former popularized survives is most evident in the florescence of that genre in the *Cantigas de Santa Maria.* The differences between the two manifestations of Marian miracles are vast, it is true, not only concerning versification, sources, and the number of miracles presented but also concerning form and presentation; but even so, the underlying theme and tone run in similar channels and the overall effect and purpose belong to the same traditions.

To understand the remarkable techniques employed to present the brief narratives of the *Cantigas de Santa Maria,* one must realize that these miracles were carefully planned and couched in three media—poetic, melodic, and visual—to catch and hold attention. Berceo's *Milagros* might have been set to music, though this has never been considered seriously to date. But brief narrative with the visual is rare. Sometimes, it is true, chronicles contain depictions of events, but these can seldom be regarded as brief narratives and certainly not as fictional brief narratives. Also scriptural and other sacred tales were painted, depicted in stained glass windows, portrayed in sculpture, or carved in wood or in other materials, and all of these could have inspired Alfonso's artists. But the illuminations in the *Cantigas,* if not the first brief fictional narratives in Spanish painting, are among the first and also among the most fertile of all medieval Spanish collections of brief narratives in painting.

Only with the threefold media of the presentations in mind can Alfonso X's sacred *Cantigas* be properly understood and evaluated. Therefore considerable treatment of each of the media must be presented before the more conventional elements of narrative technique can be assessed.

Although the *Cantigas de Santa Maria* extend the pietistic brief narrative well across the thirteenth century, and though they should be regarded as one of the great masterpieces of that century of literary and artistic activity and enlightenment, if not as the greatest, they have received only a small percentage of the attention they deserve. Without doubt, the *Cantigas* is the richest, least studied, and least understood and esteemed of the repositories of brief narrative in European literature. They are generally given short shrift in histories of Peninsular literature, histories of art have little to say about the truly gorgeous miniatures which illustrate many of the miracles, and even musicologists, with very few exceptions, have tended to overlook them. Their importance in the study of medieval folklore, daily life and customs, and even medieval history is equally great, and almost equally unperceived, and their narrative techniques have simply not been accorded any serious study at all. Why is this?

Two primary reasons have led to the omission of the *Cantigas de Santa Maria* from the study they richly deserve. The first is their linguistic vehicle, which is not Castilian, even though the songs were composed under the patronage of a Spanish monarch, and may have been written all or in part by that monarch. The second reason, no less specious, especially as regards their omission from studies in brief narrative, is that all the *Cantigas* are brief narratives in verse. Why this should have caused their omission from studies like those of Menéndez y Pelayo is difficult to say, but Berceo and the *Cantigas* nevertheless were excluded.[5] Hispanists know that in the Spanish Middle Ages virtually all lyric verse was composed in Galician-Portuguese and not in Castilian. The very paucity of medieval lyrics in Castilian proves more than anything else that poets preferred Galician to Castilian and that Spaniards understood this dialect of Portuguese. The preference for Galician would continue across the thirteenth century as well as over the two following centuries, before Castilian would come into its own as the vehicle of lyric verse. There can be no question, therefore, that when Alfonso and other poets wrote in Galician, they expected their works to be comprehended. The *Cantigas* were written to be sung publicly at court and in churches, and they were directed at all levels of society. Obviously, the king would not have couched the miracles in a language beyond the ken of those who he believed would benefit by hearing them. Many were the miracles everyone had heard in Latin or in Spanish, for example in the works of Gil de Zamora or Berceo; but many other miracles were not found in any collection, and some came from remote areas of Spain and Portugal and even from abroad or belonged entirely to folklore.[6] Such miracles would never have reached the centers of Spanish culture like Toledo, Burgos, and Seville had not King Alfonso placed them in the *Cantigas de Santa Maria.* Would the king, who had caused so many miracles to be gathered and assembled, composed in the most poetic language of the day in the favorite poetic meters, set to music and illustrated by the most lavish miniatures, have gone to so much trouble if he for a moment believed his people would not understand what they heard or read? Surely he would not have. He always labored to dignify Castilian as a language. It was he who caused it to be the vehicle of the law, the sciences, fiction, and even of diplomatic correspondence with foreign courts.[7] He believed, then, in comprehension and he surely desired that the *Cantigas de Santa Maria* be understood. That they must have been comprehended is virtually certain. Even today Spaniards can read Portuguese and understand it when they hear it spoken. In the Middle Ages, the similarities were even greater than they are today.

The *Cantigas,* then, must be considered as an integral part of a literature dear to Spaniards and readily understood by them. What these poems brought to the corpus of brief narrative in Spain can hardly be over-stressed. The king himself believed all this so firmly that he caused it to be written in his last will and testament that the *Books of Songs in Praise of Holy Mary* were to be stored in the church where his body would lie and that they were to be sung on feast days of the Virgin.[8] There in Seville's cathedral the most lavishly illustrated and illuminated volume of these songs was stored until Philip II had it removed with other treasures to enrich the library at the Escorial, and there that precious volume resides to this day.

It may seem irrelevant at this juncture to belabor the matter of authorship, especially this far into the study of the *Cantigas de Santa Maria*. And yet, in any study of literature authorship is important. In the study of Berceo it is clear that the man himself so personalized the materials he was using as his models as to produce something very close to originality. Likewise Alfonso X lives in his *Cantigas de Santa Maria* and, to a degree, perhaps even greater than in the case of Berceo in his *Milagros*. In the *Cantigas* we can see the king actually pictured, we can read one of the *Cantigas* in one of the great *cancioneiros* of a later century in which it is listed under his name and recognized as his composition, along with scores of other poems, and we know from the prologues to his works that the king oversaw and edited all the books produced under his patronage. It is therefore necessary to insist, when one speaks of the *Cantigas de Santa Maria* of Alfonso X, that these songs may well be his own compositions, either in toto or in part. It may satisfy some to believe that Alfonso merely ordered the great books of Marian miracles to be produced, with all their musical and pictorial accompaniments, and this in itself, given his propensity for editing and correcting, is a considerable accomplishment. But if he composed the four hundred-odd songs, or even if he composed some, he must be considered no longer simply as an editor and a patron, but as a literary artist in his own right, and even as an expert musician.

Scholars have noticed a consistency of style and method that points to single authorship, leading to the supposition that Alfonso himself composed the *Cantigas* and set them to music.[9] Some of the stories he may very well have collected personally,[10] while others he may have paid others to assemble for him, and, of course, when the stories derive from the great Latin repositories of miracles, these were simply hispanicized and versified. No one to my knowledge has suggested that Alfonso painted the miniatures, and since he employed painters for some artwork,[11] it is likely that he employed such men to create the miniatures of the *Cantigas,* but he could have been proficient in the art of painting. He was a most versatile man, definitely a genius, and a tireless worker.

How could the king have found the time, some will ask, to compose so much, considering how busy he was in his struggle to keep his kingdom from succumbing to the many attacks made upon it? How could he write poems and set them to music while he was editing vast historical, scientific, and legalistic compilations? And would a husband almost constantly at outs with a headstrong wife, a father whose sons revolted against him, a king who literally waged war in ecclesiastical courts against the pope himself in his attempt to gain the title of Emperor of the Holy Roman Empire, find the hours needed to compose four hundred and more hymns and songs? Even in his own times, his people leveled against him the accusation that he used too much of his time on matters that were not part of the administration of the realm. Yet no one today seems to wonder how he managed to edit and oversee the histories, the scientific works, and the preparation of the greatest legal codex in European law. Why then question his industry as a poet and musician?

Alfonso was one of those geniuses who could make time for whatever he wished to do, no matter what the expense to his health and comfort. He could, as some other geniuses have manged to do, let one task serve as a relief from another or even assume the role of relaxation or recreation. Down through the ages busy people—politicians, statesmen, warriors, rulers—have wended home, bone weary, to sit down and write books, compose poems, or write songs; others have turned to the production of furniture, to painting, to sculpture, to architecture. Another Spaniard, the Emperor Hadrian, whose economic, legalistic, militaristic, and governmental obligations far surpassed those of Alfonso X, since Hadrian ruled the western world and substantial areas of the east, found time to become an expert musician—on several instruments—to be an architect whose importance as it affected Roman, and later European, architecture is just being fully realized, to choose sculptors whose works, under the emperor's standards of taste, would shape the development of that art even into our own times, to write an autobiography (not extant), to master oratory, to excell in hunting, and to assemble a retinue of artists and art objects never before equaled.[12] No one seems to doubt these accomplishments, nor those of the Divine Julius or of Marcus Aurelius, who found time for literary activity. Hundreds of great figures in history have done so, for such is the quality of the genius. When busy people write, it is because they feel they should, or because they want to, or because something drives them to it. The causes of inspiration may be myriad—the urge to escape from mundane thoughts, to smother the horrors or the boredom of the triviality or the world, to prove that one can be aesthetic as well as practical in the world—and surely the Learned King knew one or more of these and other stimuli. Was it the desire to keep up with the competition in the area of poetry and the arts, when he had brought together so many experts in these fields of endeavor? Or did he seek to escape from the disappointments all monarchs experience, or was it to lessen the pain of disillusionment his family brought him, even to the hatefulness of a queen who never loved him? Or were the *Cantigas de Santa Maria* his great and sustained effort to prove to the Blessed Virgin that she meant more in his life than any other single being, and that, if he proved his devotion to her, she would assist him on earth and lead him, saved, into the kingdom of heaven. Alfonso was, most scholars admit, a medieval man and yet a man ahead of his time in such areas as the role all branches of learning should play in human life; but in the sphere of the soul he was entirely medieval. Like Berceo, another devotee of the Virgin; like his nephew, the worldly Don Juan Manuel or the ribald and sensual Juan Ruiz, both of whom considered themselves Our Lady's troubadours; like countless other Spaniards across the ages, this devotion to and this belief in the assistance of the Blessed Virgin, this obsession with her clemency and power, and her intervention in temporal affairs, which even today survives and leads thousands to Lourdes and Fatima, and in the New World to Guadalupe, this feeling for her could have been the inspiration that drove him to the composition of the *Cantigas de Santa Maria*. We cannot know this with certainty, of course, but since the evidence of it exists, we should not discount it because we have so different a point of view and subscribe to the tenets of so different a milieu.

After all, few people today see the Virgin Mary, have visions, or talk to eyewitnesses of miracles. Alfonso had such experiences or believed he had them. During one of his wars he decided to turn aside from conflict and visit the Monastery of Santo Domingo de Silos. There he had a vision in which he talked with Santo Domingo who told him that he would win the battle and named the day of victory.[13] While he was ruling Murcia, Alfonso saw a miracle take place and he related it in *Cantiga* 169:

E daquest' un miragre direi grande, que vi
des que mi Deus me deu Murça, e outrossi
dezir a muitos mouros que moravan ant' y
e tīian a terra por nossa pecadilla.

(8-11)

Evelyn Procter noticed an unusual preponderance of the personal life of Alfonso in the *Cantigas de Santa Maria* and in the personal lives of his family and household.[14] Were, then, some of the *Cantigas* biographical or autobiographical?

In either case the king either caused incidents from his life or his family's to be versified for the *Cantigas* or himself wrote *Cantigas* to relate events of a most personal nature which he considered to be miraculous. Considerable study should be accorded the matter of the direct role of the king in his *Cantigas de Santa Maria.*[15]

GALICIAN—THE LANGUAGE OF THE *CANTIGAS*

Some will argue that the Galician employed by Alfonso in the *Cantigas,* and indeed by all the erudite poets who wrote in that tongue—and this meant nearly all poets in Spain—was of a variety too fine, too learned, too much the property of erudition to reach the common people. The Galician of the *Cantigas,* however, was not the pleasantly flexible and mature tongue that Portuguese would be in later times, but, because it had long been in contact with and modeled upon Provençal and Catalan cultured verse, it was a language with a cultural status of its own and one respected abroad, as well as in the Peninsula. It was, it is true, a Galician refined and polished by poets into an artistic literary vehicle, with a vocabulary familiar to those who dealt with the *fin amor* of the Provençal troubadours and with phrases and syntactical elements more Provençal and Catalan than native. But even so, it never lost the flavor of popular Galician and it never became too erudite to be understood by the man on the street or in the pasture, whether in Portugal or in Spain. This should be easy for English speakers to understand. Scholars have made it clear that commoners in London and in the English provinces, too, understood and savored the lines of Shakespeare, no matter how erudite that bard might wax. It should be repeated that although a dialect, Galician was Portuguese and that people at all levels of society in Spain or Portugal must have been able to understand it. Old Spanish, Old Portuguese, and Old Galician developed simultaneously and along many similar lines, and were indeed sister tongues.

At any rate, the Galician in the *Cantigas* is simple, direct, and, though generally grammatical and correct, redolent of popular speech.[16] The verses flow with simplicity and ease allowing the miracles to unfold with admirable economy. Many are almost scripturally brief, and each follows a traditional formula or manner of presentation. Before each miracle appears a brief summary in Galician prose. In *Cantiga* 273, for example, appear these lines: "Esta e como Santa Maria deu fios a ũu ome bõo pera coser a savãa do seu altar" after which the poem begins.

Various scholars of eminence have speculated as to the reason that led the Learned King to make Galician-Portuguese the language of the *Cantigas*. Américo Castro believed the Castilian poets of the period regarded their own tongue as too harsh for lyric verse and therefore used Galician, but this view has been rejected by most modern scholars.[17] Nor do many subscribe today to the theory of C. Sánchez Albornoz, namely, that since the Castilians lived in a land at war with the Moors, they had little time for lyric verse, whereas Galicia, insofar as war and politics were concerned, was removed from such stress and strain and therefore was an area more conducive to the composition of lyric poetry.[18]

A more reasonable view may be that the Castilian court, especially in the days of Alfonso X, made it a literary convention to use the conservative and already archaizing tongue of Galicia instead of their own Castilian. Something similar had happened in France where the language of lyric verse was often Provençal rather than French, even in parts of France far away from Provence or the border between the two linguistic areas. Where the court of Eleanor of Aquitaine was in residence, Provençal was the fashion.[19] And in Spain, whether the court was in León or Galicia or Castile or Andalusia, Galician-Portuguese was the fashionable language for lyric poetry. Moreover, Galician served as a lingua franca, since poets from any linguistic area, even from France or Italy, could write their poems in Galician and be certain that they would have an audience at court and among cultured people interested in lyric poetry. Indeed, their audience might be less erudite folk, since most Spaniards, whatever their region, could comprehend Galician.

As to the making of the miniatures, it is believed that three Spanish cities had the strongest influence—Seville, Toledo, and Murcia—but that the artists were not constrained to paint in any particular place and could have produced their miniatures in a wide variety of places. This nomadlike life of the artists may explain many backgrounds in the *Cantigas* that radiate local color. In answer to the question of those who ask why the great Aqueduct of Segovia was painted with horseshoe arches rather than the Roman arches which the aqueduct contains, Guerrero Lovillo states that the Moorish arches seen everywhere in Seville are probably responsible. Either the miniaturists did not visit Segovia or they just decided to paint horseshoe arches.

With so much said about the Galician-Portuguese language of the *Cantigas,* attention of a detailed nature is due the versification itself, since the poetic structure of the songs no doubt contributed to their narrative technique. Since Galician possessed the syntactical and linguistic qualities so well suited to poetry, a variety of verse forms evolved. Not for nothing did some 200 poets leave a heritage of some 2,000 poems in the surviving *cancioneiros,* exclusive of the *Cantigas de Santa Maria.*[20]

VERSIFICATION IN THE *CANTIGAS*

Dorothy Clotelle Clarke has published the best treatment to date on the poetics of the *Cantigas de Santa Maria.*[21] So wide a range of meters did she discover in these songs that she believed that the *Cantigas* might be the possible source of all Spanish meters.

That is to say, that Alfonso's ability to select, at almost the dawn of Peninsular formal poetry, lasting qualities in so intricate an art as that of versification is indeed admirable. All presently known verse forms employed in Castilian before the Golden Age are found in the *Cantigas.* And there is in the collection a foreshadowing, as Menéndez y Pelayo indicates, of the Golden Age and modern times. Alfonso's system of verse measure—syllable count—was the one followed almost exactly in subsequent Castilian poetry. Alfonso's rhythmic patterns have lived to the present time and his strophe forms could have been prototypes for a number of basic Castilian strophes. His great fondness for polymetric combinations is of particular significance.[22]

The most frequently employed verse form in the *Cantigas* is the Arabic *zéjel* or the Proveçal *virelai.* In both, a brief strophe states the theme, usually in the form of a couplet (*Cantiga* 273). The following citation and all others come from the definitive edition of the *Cantigas* by Walter Mettmann.

A Madre de Deus, que éste do mundo lum' e espello,
sempre nas cousas minguadas acorre e dá conssello.
(1-2)

Then the *Cantiga* continues in strophes frequently of five monorhymed verses, the last of which must always be the first verse of the original couplet:

Desta razon um miragre   direy apost' e fremoso,
que fezo Santa María,   e d' oyr mui soboroso;
esto foi en Ayamonte,   logar ja quanto fragoso,
pero terra avondada   de perdiz e de cõello.
A Madre de Deus que éste do mundo lum' e espello.
(5-9)

It should be noted in passing, touching the matter of the Arabic *zéjel,* that this verse form may or may not be of Arabic origin. Some scholars hold that it is a Mozarab folk form borrowed by Arabic poets in Andalusia from their Mozarab subjects (Christian Spaniards who lived under Arabic rule and sometimes spoke Arabic).[23] The form is known also to have been present from early times in Hebrew and Christian liturgies; that parallels exist also in the *virelai* of Provençal literature, as well as in the Catalonian *goig* and the Castilian *villancico,* is not surprising. But whether the Christian folk of Andalusia originated the form and gave it to their Arabic overlords, or whether it was created by the Andalusian Moorish poets, it was a form that spread and was much used and loved.

Perhaps the most typical type of *zéjel,* then, contains a thematic refrain which in Spanish is known as the *estribillo,* and this is repeated before each strophe. Sometimes in the *Cantigas* the *estribillo* contains two or more verses, since so wide a variety of this aspect of versification is present. The length of line varies enormously, even astonishingly. *Cantiga* 276, for example, contains but seven syllables, while *Cantiga* 5 has sixteen. The favorite, however, contained eight, and to this day the octosyllabic line is the most popular in Spanish poetry.

Gilbert Chase, who has made significant studies of Spanish metrics and music, believes that two *estribillos* were of special popularity. "Many of them consist of four-line stanzas (rhyme scheme *b b b a*), with a refrain in the form of a rhymed couplet (*a a*) coming before and after each stanza." He recognized, too, the frequency of "the four-line refrain (*a b a b*) and a six-line stanza with alternating rhyme."²⁴

A well-known and studied long-lined *estribillo* can be found in *Cantiga* 5:

> Quena coitas deste mundo ben quiser soffrer,
> Santa Maria deve sempr' antesi pōer.

Another is exemplified in *Cantiga* 11:

> Macar ome per folia
> aginna caer
> pod' en pecado
> do ben de Santa Maria
> non dev' a seer
> desesperado
> (1-6)

Still more variety can occur in the *zéjel,* as Dorothy Clotelle Clarke points out. Even alternating rhyme which replaces the monorhymed sequences occurs. And sometimes new rhymes are inserted between the original monorhymed lines—*a b a b a b a c, d e d e d e c*) (see *Cantigas* 156, 157, 180). Others use still longer monorhymed sequences, as in the case of *Cantigas* 95 and 283. Clarke states, "Among the strophes less popular with Alfonso el Sabio in the *Cantigas,* but which became strophes of primary importance in Castilian are: the *redondilla*—though not octosyllabic in the *Cantigas* (Nos. 230, 326, p. 589); the *pareado* (No. 260); the *copla de pie quebrado* (No. 300); monorhymed quatrains similar to the *cuaderna vía* strophe but having different lines (p. 599); a form closely resembling the *romancillo* (No. 401); and above all, a *romance* (No. 308)."²⁵ It is interesting to note the *romance* form, the earliest known manifestation extant, inasmuch as it would become the major vehicle for narrative poetry in the ballad which has never ceased to enrich Spanish poetry.

In the typical *zéjel,* the *estribillo* in the last verse sets the pattern of rhyme for the last verse in the strophe. *Cantiga* 144 illustrates this well. The *estribillo* is given below in italics:

Con razon e d'averen gran pavor
as bestias da Madre daquel Sennor
que sobre todas cousas á *poder.*
E dest' un gran miragre foi mostrar
Santa Maria, a Virgen sen par,
en Prazença, per com' oy contar
a omees bōos et de *creer.*   (3-9)

The most important, according to Clarke, were the hendecasyllable and then the heptasyllable, but the latter should not be confused with the Italianate form given much renown later by Garcilaso. To continue, there are examples of twelve-syllable lines (*Cantigas* 123, 145, 209, 223) and of fourteen-syllable lines (*Cantiga* 16); Dorothy Clarke reveals that *Cantiga* 240 contains a very rare accent on the fourth syllable, while 211 is accented consistently on the fifth; occasionally verse form changes within a poem. Something closely resembling *arte mayor,* most current in the fifteenth century, appears in number 79 and 307, and the only difference between the Alfonsine *arte mayor* and that of later times lies in the regularity of syllable count in the *Cantigas.* Still other metrical forms, not seen in Castilian poetry until the late nineteenth century, can be seen in *Cantigas* 25 and 73.

Clarke finds, "The shortest line used as the sole verse-length in a poem is the hexasyllable, which appears in both the patterns later found in Castilian, particularly during and after the Golden Age: the *seranilla* (No. 192) having fluctuating secondary accent."[26] She indicates, too, that there are examples of the decasyllable (*Cantigas* 15, 20, 280), of the fourteen-syllable (12, 23, and others), and the fifteen-syllable in 36.[27]

The rhyme of the *Cantigas* is pure consonance rather than assonance, and in rhyme pattern something like near perfection prevails because a pattern set down in the first strophe is faithfully continued in all the other strophes. Rhyme scheme, it goes without saying, is rich and varied. Those *Cantigas* which appear to lack artistry, as one reads them, will be seen to regain it, if one hears them sung as musical notation directs, for the words under the control of the notes fall into an artistic pattern. No small part of this can be explained by the employment of enjambement.

Anna Chisman's study of versification in the *Cantigas,* especially as it relates to enjambement, emphasizes this hitherto little studied phenomenon. After making it plain, as had Dorothy Clotelle Clarke, how strictly metrical the poems are, Anna Chisman writes: "In contrast, the *Cantigas* are striking in the loose 'fit' of grammatical clause to poetic line: there is constant and heavy use of enjambement, even between strophes, with the intervention of a refrain. The extreme lack of concern that a line be co-terminus with a complete grammatical construction is quite unprecedented in the vernacular poetry of Spain and France in the late Middle Ages."[28]

Since enjambement plays so important a role in the *Cantigas* one wonders how the usage affects narrative technique. Chisman reveals that enjambement, while it may sometimes cloud meaning when it violates grammar by breaking up syntax groups, nevertheless simultaneously causes surprise and focuses attention. This is an unexpected narrative technique and a novel one indeed. Caesura enjambement, Chisman states, is another technique in narration. It concentrates the hearer's or reader's attention upon words which are critical to the narrative. Attention-binding is a critical goal in storytelling, and this particular technique is noteworthy. But even more important is the fact that "enjambement also has other effects on the narrative poems: it increases the pace and introduces a certain freedom and variety into the strict form."[29] Since the *loores* were not primarily narrative poems, and usually had no narrative movement at all, it is not surprising that they use very little enjambement, making their lyric style correspondingly different. This contrast, as pointed out by Chisman in her dissertation, emphasizes that enjambement was certainly reserved for narrative poems for the very reason that enjambement pertains to the narrative rather than the lyric, at least in the *Cantigas de Santa Maria*. Apparently, then, enjambement is a definite and carefully planned aspect of versified narrative and one deliberately established for narrating the miracles of Our Lady in the Alfonsine *Cantigas*. Probably the narrative value of enjambement has been described more clearly by Chisman than by anyone, as her statement that "the accumulation of enjambement which gives the impression of bursting the barriers of a constraining form and produces the effect of rapid, artless story-telling, of casual conversation in which it is the story, rather than the manner of telling it which dominates," makes very clear.[30]

This subtle technique, scarcely noticed or even sensed by the audience, whether visual or aural, is remarkable in any age. To find it in the Alfonsine period is startling, indeed.

THE MUSIC OF THE *CANTIGAS*

With so facile a versification and such a rich linguistic organ as Galician to support it, it is no wonder that the melodic variation and excellence of the *Cantigas de Santa Maria* mark these songs as medieval lyrics par excellence. Only a very learned musicologist of the twentieth century can explain the intricacies of the music of the *Cantigas de Santa Maria*. But even the layman who hears the excellent modern interpretations of the songs can sense the power they must have exerted over those who heard them in the Middle Ages.[31] That they contributed to narrative technique will be demonstrated subsequently. It is believed that the king himself was no mean musician. Even if he had not been a musician, he would have been a devotee of music. What Gilbert Chase says about Spanish monarchs and Alfonso X specifically, as concerns music, certainly is correct. "It is known that Spanish kings and nobles employed Moorish-Arabian musicians in their palaces. Some of the miniatures of the *Cantigas* of Alfonso the Wise of Castile, for example, show Moorish musicians playing various instruments together with Spanish musicians."[32]

If the miniatures reveal the truth, as surely they must, then Alfonso imported and employed many troubadours and *juglares* from Europe as well as from Moorish Spain, Moorish North Africa, and even from the Levant. To support Chase's statement one need only view the illustration for the second of the two prologues of Codex T.1.I (sometimes referred to as Escorial 1 or E-I), whose title reads *Esta é a primeira cantiga de loor de Santa Maria, ementando os VII goyos que ouve de seu Fillo.* The king is clearly portrayed seated in the center of the picture, facing the viewer. He is engaged in turning the pages of a book on a writing desk beside him, while he explains as a teacher might. Seated almost at his feet to the left is a tonsured clerical scribe, who is writing; also seated on the floor, to the right, is a secular scribe. The words and score of a song are visible on the scrolls in the hands of the scribes. At the far right of the picture stand four clerics, one holding an open book so that the other three may read it. They seem to be singing. At the far left stand three musicians tuning their fiddles, as they seem to await the king's signal to play. Here, just as in a different miniature mentioned by Gilbert Chase, one can view what many scholars believe is an actual pictorial account of the king as he dictates a song to his scribes while four singers vocalize it and three musicians prepare to contribute their instrumental interpretation. The value of a picture like this to an understanding of the very processes of song making and song presentation with musical accompaniment is inestimable. In passing, it should be mentioned that in still another codex of the *Cantigas de Santa Maria* are contained pictures of seventy-odd musicians, both Christian and Moslem, playing their instruments which include a wide variety of the percussion type, numerous members of the strings such as lutes, forerunners of the viol, and guitars, harps, a hurdy-gurdy, several varieties of organ, recorders, sets of silver bells and timbrels, lutes, drums, bagpipes, castanets, some reed instruments, and numerous varieties of horns and trumpets.[33]

Certainly the melodies of the *Cantigas* stem from many sources. Some are obviously from sacred music—Alfonsine musicians could draw upon the Mozarabic liturgies which still survived in spite of the Church's insistence upon its own rite. The noted musicologist Saville Clark, dealing with the types and sources of the melodies of the *Cantigas,* writes:

Of course the *Cantigas* use many different kinds of melody, as any examination of the collection must show. It would seem some—a very large number—derive from western chant; a large number seem to have an indirect relation to chant but have been transformed by a uniquely Spanish kind of lyricism; a few clearly derive from popular songs; but a large group, perhaps the largest of all, have no relation to chant whatsoever, nor can they be analyzed according to the western modal system. It would seem reasonable to assume that these melodies were composed with Arab models in mind, and that some of them may even be Arabic melodies; further, that what we hear as uniquely Spanish lyricism is due, at least in part, to the presence of Arabs in Spain for over 500 years before these songs were written.[34]

Gilbert Chase wrote of Moorish and Arabic musicians, and among the illustrations of musicians found in one of the codices of the *Cantigas de Santa Maria* are many Moslems. And yet, Higinio Anglés stated that the *Cantigas* have nothing to do with Arabic music, so the experts differ. A ground for explaining these divergences of opinion may be the "popular" derivation, and this will be touched upon below.[35]

The chants of the western Church are familiar enough to most educated people to make it easy to detect these backgrounds for *Cantigas* based upon them; but for popular songs, it may be wiser to think in terms of secular songs, a classification which may embody a wide variety of melodies. What were popular songs in Alfonso's times and from what roots did they spring? Native "Spanish" songs from before the coming of the Moors certainly existed, and thirteenth-century Spanish popular songs may have been sung when Alfonso began to produce the *Cantigas*. The Arabs, as Clark reminded us, had been in Spain for 500 years before the *Cantigas* were written, and therefore Arabic songs may well have formed part of the native, non-Moorish "Spanish" folk music and indeed might not have been recognized by the folk as Arabic songs after the passage of the years; the same might be said of Hebrew melodies. Provençal troubadours had entered Spain and Portugal before Alfonso's time and continued to visit Spain while the *Cantigas* were being composed. At first troubadour songs may have been heard at court and among erudite people, principally among poets. Songs, however, like other elements of erudite life, often filter down to the common people. And not to be forgotten are the types of singers who would not have been received at court or by the erudite—common poets who could have come to Spain from France or Provence or, for that matter, from a number of other places. Untold thousands of pilgrims had traveled to Compostela from many parts of Europe and the British Isles, among them Chaucer's earthy Wife of Bath, as she herself tells us in her story. It is intriguing likewise to speculate upon the influence of those musicians and singers who must have accompanied the royal brides of Spanish monarchs. Alfonso's father married Beatriz of Suabia; in her retinue came musicians and singers and composers from the Germanies. Alfonso's half-sister, Leanor, wed the English prince who would reign as Edward I. What songs from England might she not have sent to her musically inclined relative in Spain? Louis IX was Alfonso's second cousin and he was given a copy of the *Cantigas* by Alfonso, leading one to speculate as to what literary gifts might have been given in return. Alfonso's own wife Violante was the daughter of King James of Aragon and the sister of King Bela of Hungary. Other royal marriages could have brought musicians from such places as Hungary, Constantinople, Rumania, and Norway.

In the sphere of popular melodies, then, Spain was rich, and King Alfonso had a vast reservoir of songs upon which the draw: the chanteys of sailors from a welter of European, Mideastern, and African ports; the songs of harvesters, shepherds, hunters, fishermen, and *vaqueros;* soldier ballads; and the songs of watchmen and the sometimes ribald songs of the wandering scholars. "The interplay of popular and artistic elements," wrote Chase, "has nowhere been more significantly revealed than in

Spanish music."[36] The statement is quite applicable to the *Cantigas de Santa Maria*. And the relevance of so many strains to the very fiber of narrative technique is startling. A miracle about shepherds might well have been set to a folk melody from the repertory of shepherd songs; those miracles which relate the adventures of pilgrims on the way to or traveling from Compostela might have been set to the strains of pilgrim songs; miracles at sea and miracles on the battlefield could have been derived from well-known chanteys and from war songs. We can never know, of course, since what was a war song in the thirteenth century might have survived as a quite different kind of song.

The influence of the *Cantigas* themselves after Alfonso's death has not been traced. The king bequeathed the songs to the Cathedral of Seville with the command that they be sung on feast days of the Virgin, and at least one of the codices (the Escorial manuscript) remained in that cathedral until Philip II had it removed and archived at the Escorial.[37] Probably the *Cantigas* were actually sung on Our Lady's feast days in Seville, just as they are occasionally sung today. But none of this means that the individual *Cantigas* had much circulation. Quite probably after Alfonso's death, many never escaped the ecclesiastical library and most, therefore, lay in oblivion. Certainly no one of scholarly pretensions studied them effectively or evaluated them until the present century, since those who studied the codices in the nineteenth century failed to understand how the musical scores were to be interpreted. As was at first true in the handling of the songs of the Provençal troubadours, no one could fathom the true beauty concealed behind a system of musical notation simply beyond the faulty understanding of the investigators. Even in the early twentieth century the well-known musicologist Julián Ribera could not capture, or so the most up-to-date studies would suggest, the full flavor of these songs. His belief that virtually all, if not all, the melodies came from Arabic music is no longer in vogue. And so it is only recently that what can be described as a reliable reading of Alfonsine music came into being.

A musicologist of world renown and remarkable erudition, Higinio Anglés, who was moved by a sense of Spanish pride and the determination to solve the mystery of the notation in the *Cantigas de Santa Maria,* finally unraveled the problems. He wrote, and I translate, "The repertory of the 423 *Cantigas de Santa Maria,* as presented in the extant texts, is to the present time the most important repertory in Europe as regards medieval sacred lyric. The melodies have no relationship at all with the oriental music of the Arabs. . . . The notation of the *Cantigas* . . . is almost perfect, although until very recently it has been unknown by musicologists."[38]

Anglés, then, has at last refuted the unfortunate opinion of many musicologists who have, in their confusion, stated that the songs are of poor quality. Their error arose because it was universally believed that these *Cantigas* could be transcribed in accordance with modern rules of musical notation. When Anglés finally realized that no established regulation of musicology could be obeyed, insofar as the notation of the *Cantigas* was concerned, he realized that the approach to its full understanding could only be had by a return to the original thirteenth-century codices. Once he had made this decision, he was able to develop certain techniques of his own which made it possible at last to transcribe what the medieval musicians had penned. With confidence, he could state, "The Alfonsine *cantigas* contain a melodic richness and a rhythmic variety not found in any other European repository."[39] This is a strong statement, but one which musicologists today consistently accept. It must be stressed, then, that in the realm of music, too, as well as in verse, the *Cantigas de Santa Maria* are unique and important to a degree that is still not fully comprehended.

It is to Anglés primarily that we owe an understanding of the relationship between medieval music and European folk song, and especially Peninsular folk song. Among the hundreds of popular songs he studied, Anglés discovered many, sung to this day, which contain the same wealth of melody and in some cases even the same forms and melodies preserved in the *Cantigas de Santa Maria*. "In them [that is, in the *Cantigas de Santa Maria*]," he writes, "the rhythmic element of the folk song rules, as we do not find it in the lyrics of the troubadours and minnesingers."[40] Going deeper into the matter of actual notation, he wrote, "Specialists had believed until recently that medieval monody must have had a close relationship with the polyphony of its epoch, and, since in this polyphony only the ternary measure was practiced, this rhythm alone was possible in the monody. But the notation of the *Cantigas* reveals just the opposite. In them is presented the ternary measure which combines with the binary; again melodies exist which can be sung with only the binary."[41]

When the studies of Anglés have had the circulation and influence they merit, his discoveries may have even more relevance to the history of musicology than the recent investigations of the music of the troubadours. The music of the latter, like that of the Alfonsine *Cantigas,* had obeyed, it was believed, the rules governing the meter and rhyme of medieval polyphony. And because scholars had believed, and many still do believe, that polyphony is the only key to understanding these meters and rhymes, they failed to realize that it was a mistake to apply the same rules to monody. They had searched in vain for years for some medieval manuscript from which might come a clue or an actual guide to the comprehension of monody. Anglés, almost caustically, states, "These manuscripts which we looked for and never found, have just been discovered: they are the Spanish manuscripts of the Court of Castile and León; they are the manuscripts of the *Cantigas* of Alfonso el Sabio."[42]

Only a trained musicologist can follow the professional interpretations of the *Cantigas* found in Anglés's definitive work. But even a layman can comprehend something of the magnitude and relevance of his studies.

Musical presentation, used to illustrate the narration, was very much part of the *Cantigas de Santa Maria.* Everyone knows, of course, that music as a vehicle for story is as old as story itself, and that quite probably songs which told stories may have been the earliest of narratives in most cultures, if not in all, no matter how primitive. It is known that bards chanted war songs and other epics as did later troubadours and scops. Then as now brief narratives, especially those set to music, charmed and attracted most. A convincing test is a comparison, for example, between a reading of *Barbara Allen* and a musical rendition of the same ballad.

In Spanish no brief narratives set to music survive before the thirteenth century, but evidence supports the existence of musical stories much earlier. The now famous *jarchas*—the earliest extant of which date from the eleventh century, although they are undoubtedly much older—were very early Romance or Spanish lyrics and were presumably love lyrics sung by peasant girls.[43] That erudite Hebrew and Arabic poets in Andalusia borrowed crucial lines from these folk songs to add to their love poems, and that the parts borrowed were hardly narratives, does not preclude the existence of lyrical narratives. Perhaps narrative, balladlike pieces existed. And hymns in Spanish may have existed from quite early times, although the presence of Church Latin hymns might well have curtailed Spanish songs of the same kind. Other sacred songs, or melodies related to pious matters, some of which might have been narrative or seminarrative quite possibly existed. One remembers the *Quem quaeritis* tropes or the early beginnings of such religious dramas as the Elche play whose origins extend far back in time. Both varieties contain a small kernel of story. Certainly church drama in Latin, as well as hymns, the Mass itself, which is dramatic and seminarrative, and such sequences as those found in the *Peristephanon* of Prudentius (died ca. 405), a series of hymns of definitely narrative character recounting the deeds and the sufferings of martyrs, were highly esteemed.

Alfonso could have dipped into a number of reservoirs of musical narrative in search of models and suggestions for his *Cantigas de Santa Maria* and could have chosen strains which had relevance to the songs which is not possible for us to recognize today. The Learned King knew well that familiarity, in the case of good melodies, does not breed contempt, but on the contrary attracts and delights. A miracle set to a popular and esteemed melody, whether that melody were secular or clerical, could, he knew, develop a very special degree of rapport. Moreover, it could fix the miracle couched in such a melody in the people's minds, since it could be hummed or sung or whistled. The importance of this to the method of telling a story, to the content of the story, and to the remembrance and longevity of the story is obvious. The pace or tempo, the choice of instrumental accompaniment, the kind of voice or voices chosen could all have been used cleverly to produce desired effects. A *Cantiga* like number 36 exemplifies the value of movement in the presentation of an exciting or breathtaking adventure. There the rhythm is striking and even compelling, and it carries the almost frenzied action rapidly forward. This is a far cry from the placid and plaintive melodies to which the less violent miracles are set. Since the musical notation of the thirteenth century bore no indication of tempo, it is therefore necessary to theorize to some extent as to how rapidly or how slowly a piece of music was to be sung or played. Only a musicologist of considerable experience can read such a notation and then play or sing the song at a tempo he believes is in consonance with its pace in the Middle Ages. Still, a *Cantiga* like number 36, to musicologists today, seems to demand a near precipitous movement, and it has been so rendered by Saville Clark for *Music of the Middle Ages*,[44] who opines that quite probably it is a folk melody. As this *Cantiga* is rendered, and especially as it applies to pace or tempo, it might be a tune that formed part of the repertoire of folk dance. One can dance to it today, if he is sufficiently agile.

With reference to tempo, and before continuing with the matter of *Can-*

tiga 36, some pertinent, and, I hope, not too naive, questions may be asked. If the funeral march or *America* or our national anthem were increased in tempo by several degrees, so that they reached that of, say, *Dixie* or *De Camptown Races,* would the effect be favorable? Would the slowly paced melodies thus rendered "sound right" and please listeners? Could a Gregorian chant have been increased in tempo successfully in the thirteenth century or could it be today? Probably the answer to all these questions is negative. Therefore, what follows, as concerns certain *Cantigas* and their melodies in relation to their narrative presentation may not be too far from actuality.

Possibly some of the *Cantigas* were accompanied by dancing. The idea is not too farfetched. Brief narratives as danced are represented by some of the present-day Spanish *jotas* which in a simple way tell a story.

But to return to the matter of number 36's melody, much can be demonstrated as to the importance of melody and its relation to subject matter. The plot of this *Cantiga* demands movement and needs a strain capable of arousing and sustaining excitement. A storm is at its height, danger and even death to all on board a ship bound for Brittany is imminent. Prayers have been said to all the saints, except the Virgin, and said in vain, and unless aid comes quickly all will be lost. The melody is such that it pulls the audience along in wild career as the events unfold. The language is terse, the lines of fifteen and sixteen syllables reminiscent of lines of prose. The reader or listener is made to hear the crew *gemendo e chorando,* to catch their words raised in vain supplication to the saints, *muito lles rogando.* Then, in the midst of the tempest is heard the voice of a cleric, critical, severe, insistent. Instantly (" 'Quand' est oyeron") the men ("todos dun coraçon e duna voontad") called upon the Holy Virgin, and their very words are recorded in a frenzied plea ("Sennor, val-nos, ca a nave sse sume!"). Even as they utter the words, they see on the top of the mast a great light and realize that the moment it appeared the wind died, the sky brightened, and the sea calmed.

Adverbs like *quand* ("When" in the sense of "as soon as"), *enton* ("right then"), and *pois* ("as soon as"), with the vibrant present participial phrase *e deziendo esto* ("on saying this") are used as effectively as the melody which carries the words. This *Cantiga* is a moving, straightforward piece, textually as well as musically. Language, vivid imagery, and insistent, driving melody blend to produce striking effects. If the singers were also actors, pantomiming, with or without stage settings, the overall impact of such a miracle could have been a moving experience. The miracle, as seen *au vif*, if indeed some of these miracles were presented dramatically, or even if seen in the miniatures of a book, and combined with the melodic and the poetic, could have stimulated any medieval audience or reader deeply.

Another swiftly moving *Cantiga* is number 205, also, according to Saville Clark, of popular vintage. The theme is secular, save for the actual miraculous occurrence. The audience learns that on the frontier a Moorish castle is under siege by a Spanish host from Uclés and Calatrava. Don Alfonso Télez has assembled fine knights, and considerable detail about the army is given, all of which the Learned King must have realized would catch the attention of those who heard the song.

> Que tragia gran conpanna   de mui bõos cavalleiros,
> ardidos e arrizados   e demais bõos guerreiros
> e almogavares muitos   peões e baesteiros,
> per que o castelo todo   muit' agȳa foi entrado.

When all but one tower is taken, the defenders go there and try to extinguish the fires that the Spaniards have lit. Events transpire quickly, as they would actually in the violent ending of a siege.

The story then reveals that a Moorish woman fled up to the very top of the tower, her baby son in her arms.

> E entre duas amēas   se foi a sentar a mesquȳa
> con seu fillo pequenȳo   que en seus braços tīia;
> e pero mui gran fogo   de todas partes viynna,
> a moura non foi queimada   nen seu fillo chamuscado.

The tower will fall; the woman is beyond rescue. As they look up, the Spanish knights see her seated in the battlements, and she reminds them of images they have seen of the Madonna and the Child. Moved by the picture, all lift their arms in prayer to the Virgin, invoking her aid for the Mooress. Then the miracle: the tower crashes in flame and ruin, but the Mooress and her son miraculously, without a scratch, come to rest in a meadow. Of course, the *Cantiga* ends with what the audience might have expected:

> e a moura foi crischāa   e seu fillo batiçado.

The music has been carefully transcribed by Higinio Anglés. But those who prefer to hear a fine rendition may listen to the recording of the voice of Russell Oberlin.[45]

One would have to spend much time listening to renditions of the *Cantigas* or studying their musical notations to ascertain whether or not there is anything like consistency in melodic handling for exciting miracles and for miracles of more peaceful theme. But even auditing the twelve selections in the album cited, together with the twelve in another album by Pro Musica, a few of which correspond to *Cantigas* in the first mentioned album, and taking into consideration the selections in the album produced by The Waverly Consort and that issued by the Musical Heritage Society can lead one to believe that such consistency exists.

An example of a more tender and less violent theme is *Cantiga* 118 which Saville Clark thinks may be more directly derived from an Arabic melody.[46] In this *Cantiga* we hear of no tempests or sieges, but only of a poor mother whose first three children had been stillborn in spite of her prayers and the donations she made in the form of waxen images of a child. When her fourth child was born dead the mother carried the body to Our Lady's chapel in Saragossa and begged that it be resurrected. The miracle ends with the woman's taking the living child to the shrine at Salas.

The melody of this *Cantiga* is soft and sweet, like a lullaby, rising and falling as it progresses unhurriedly with its inspiring message. The strains of number 36 would be discordant as the musical background of this miracle.

Number 97, according to Clark, is a Spanish adaptation of the western chant.[47] The mood seems to be one of comfort as the words relate how a king's man was accused behind his back of crimes against the monarch. In it one reads of no violence. Instead is revealed the man's consternation and grief and fear as he is summoned before the king. His prayers to the Virgin and the fine garment he placed in her shrine won him her favor and his accusers were confounded. Four stanzas of the twelve are the words that passed between the man and the king. The poem, then, deals with a more commonplace matter and needs no stirring melody to bring it to the audience. Even the punishment of the evildoers is no more than the disdain of the court. It is a calm little tale. Even its four-line introductory stanza, which is, of course, the refrain that terminates the stanzas, labels it immediately as one of the quieter miracles:

A Virgen sempr' acorrer,
acorrer
vai o coitad', e valer,
e valer.

Cantiga 7 is the story of an abbess whom the devil tempted into fornication with the Bolognese who was in charge of providing supplies for the convent. It is a sorrowful story and not one of those which makes fun of errant ecclesiastics. The abbess was most repentant, she went to the Virgin's altar and fell asleep crying there. Then, as though in a dream, the Virgin delivered the abbess's child and had him reared in another place; and when the bishop examined the abbess for signs of pregnancy, requiring her to undress before him, he discovered no reason to believe she had been pregnant. The *Cantiga* ends as the bishop praises God and scolds the nuns for accusing their abbess. Instead of excitement, the reader finds a psychological situation fraught with embarrassment, guilty conscience, and genuine contrition. The Virgin in her tender mercy saves the abbess from disgrace. In this Alfonsine version there is none of the harshness directed at the nuns by the bishop, for the *Cantiga* ends with no more than a scolding, differing considerably from the rendition of Berceo.

Here again the melody is a transformation of the western chant. It fits the miracle of the pregnant abbess and with its churchly ring it would have sounded in the medieval ear like a hymn.[48]

Number 364, which Saville Clark believes belongs to the type of melody more directly based upon Arabic models, is performed in a slow and soft manner.[49] Its introductory verses, and therefore its refrain, soars in a paean as it proclaims how Our Lady's devotees need fear no danger. It is a homely story of everyday life and it could have happened anywhere. There are no tempests or battles. The verses relate that thirty workmen, whose labor was given voluntarily to the building of a church to be dedicated to the Virgin, are suddenly buried when a tower constructed on soft ground topples upon them. No one is hurt, however, and after the accident they work with even greater enthusiasm to complete the church.

Music, then, is one of the facets of Alfonsine narrative technique in the *Cantigas de Santa Maria* which imparts a sophistication and charm unlike any other stories in the Peninsula during the thirteenth and fourteenth centuries. A proper choice of tempo and interpretation for each melody will reinforce and heighten the effect of the story, and conversely clues to finding the correct tempo and interpretation for each *Cantiga* can be found in the narration itself. The entire subject has not been touched, and in fact these cursory and unprofessional remarks may be the only treatment of the music of the *Cantigas* as a facet of their narrative technique.

PICTORIAL ILLUSTRATION IN THE *CANTIGAS*

The third medium, the pictorial, has never enjoyed the investigation it deserves concerning narrative technique, and this is a considerable lacuna in an important aspect of the history of the short story in Spain. Any study of narrative techniques which does not consider the miniatures in the *Cantigas* will simply be one-sided and incomplete, since they form a definite and important link between the graphic and the literary arts.

In two of the manuscripts of the *Cantigas* the miracles and the songs of praise face pages of richly illuminated miniatures which depict the action, but the most lavishly illustrated is manuscript T.1.I, now archived in the Escorial Museum.[50] The pages are large, measuring 490 millimeters in height by 326 in width. In all but a few of the *Cantigas,* the illustrated pages are divided into six panels, each framed by a frieze of brilliantly colored designs, and all the panels are enclosed in a wider margin of the same design. The few exceptions are divided into eight. The closest modern parallels to the arrangement are to be found in comic strips and children's books in which the pictorial balances or exceeds the print. Each panel has its own caption which in the briefest terms explains the picture. The songs of praise, which are not narratives in that they are not miracles, likewise follow this pattern, each panel having its own label or caption. An example follows. In *Cantiga* 11 is the first caption, "Como o monge dizia Ave Maria ant'o altar," and in the miniature the monk can be seen on his knees; the second is "Como o monge abriu as portas por ir a ssa barragana"; moving back to the left and the third panel, we read "Como o monge morreu no rio e os diaboos lle levaron a alma"; the fourth panel is labeled "Como Sancta Maria tolleu a alma do monge a os diaboos"; panel five, again on the left, reads "Como Santa Maria ressocitou o monge"; the last panel of the six is labeled "Como os monges loaron todos a Santa Maria." In these six concise statements lies the outline of the narrative, which in its entirety runs to three printed pages in the edition of Walter Mettmann and, to stay within the framework of the original, to ninety-six lines.[51] Surely not many, if any, illiterate people were ever allowed to handle so precious a book as the royal manuscript of the *Cantigas de Santa Maria,* but people at court who did peruse the book had a convenient and quick summary or sketch of each miracle. Possibly the king, or Queen Violante, when she was sufficiently at peace with her husband to be at court, might have turned the pages of the *Cantigas* for their children, reading the captions instead of the entire poem. At any rate, in the miniatures the pictorial rendition of the miracles is wedded to the simple captions, and for those who did not wish to absorb the complete account, an encapsulated version was available.

It should be added here that even though the pages of illustrations are all carefully divided into six or eight panels, the number of events depicted is not limited to six or even to eight.[52] Some panels are divided themselves by various means to depict additional incidents. Panel number 4 in *Cantiga* 9 shows what at first glance might be taken for two monks, the first of whom is facing a lion, the second a band of armed robbers. Actually, what the artist intended to be understood is the same monk facing the lion in one of his adventures and the robbers in another. If one looks closely he will see that the two confrontations are divided by a craggy rock and a line of trees. Similarly a wall and a column in the fourth panel in *Cantiga* 64 serve to divide two separate scenes.

From time to time, probably to provide greater dimension or to contribute to continuity in a miniature, the characters—animal, human, divine, or infernal—may transgress the limits of the frame separating two panels or even move outside the frieze which frames the entire page of panels. Charles Nelson quite correctly, in describing *Cantiga* 119, states:

Panel Four is so closely connected with the action of Panel Three that the two can be treated almost as one drawing. These two panels combined are probably the most outstanding of the *Cantigas* as to related actions, continuity and visualization. The chief demon is shown on the rooftop directing the capture of the High Judge and, at the same moment of time, is shown directing the demons and their disposal of the Judge in Panel Four. . . . This is an astonishingly high level of achievement in the art of animation for the thirteenth century. What appears in the pictorial art parallels exactly the narrative hook or the transition used in the poems themselves.[53]

Another example of almost equal relevance to transition can be found in *Cantiga* 63 in which a battle is being fought. The event taking place in

Panel 3 (the Virgin in the armor of a Christian knight charging the enemy) is continued directly into Panel 4, as though no line of separation, as provided by the frieze between the two panels, existed. One sees the hindquarters of the Virgin's horse in Panel 3 and its foreparts, together with most of its rider, in Panel 4. This unusual visual transition is decidedly graphic and effective. In a book where verbal enjambement is so common it is not strange to find a kind of visual enjambement almost equally prevelant. The investigation of this is a desideratum, since the phenomenon in the *Cantigas* is common and a full understanding of it would contribute to the history of brief narrative in pictorial form.

All the miniatures in the two manuscripts which portray miracles, as well as in the one which portrays only musicians and their instruments (a fourth with no illustrations whatever exists), are polychromatic. Most of the shades of red, from scarlet and crimson to plum, appear; the blues are particularly fine, ranging from deep cobalt to pale azure; yellows are frequent, especially for wheat fields and the barren slopes of mountains; greens abound, some so deep that they appear at first glance to be black, while others depict realistically the various shades of the leaves of plants and trees and greensward; browns and blacks, frequently paired with white, notably in the vestments of priests and nuns, are common; illumination in gold is lavishly present to set off crosses, altar pieces, columns, archways, and windows in churches, lamps, crowns, haloes, golden bedsteads, and tables in royal palaces, and, in short, whatever might be spotlighted with the brilliance of gold. The golden illuminations so treasured by medieval people were possible through the use of gold beaten into almost diaphanous sheets which could be cut to pattern and affixed to the portions of the manuscripts where they were needed. A coat of Armenian bole, a kind of reddish clay beneath the gold leaf, imparted a special glow which was extremely effective.

Each miniature was probably the result of the work of more than a single artist. Calligraphers set down the caption; apprentices probably did such mechanical work as drawing the friezes of the miniatures and painting the colors into these friezes; still other apprentices probably sketched some of the conventional backgrounds and scenery. One would suspect that the major artists themselves sketched in the first charcoal outlines and thereby created the skeletal framework for the painting and illuminating to follow. Fortunately the Florentine Manuscript is unfinished, to the extent that in some pages of illustrations one finds no more than the charcoal sketches mentioned above; in others some of the paint and gold has been laid on, with other parts untouched or in varying stages of production. A few of the miniatures in this manuscript reveal that the artists who painted the hands and faces of the characters, must have been the last to work, since one can see miniatures complete in all other aspects save faces and hands. One can see knights in all their robes or in their armor, mounted on their horses, with their caps or helmets in place, beneath which is a vacant spot awaiting the specialist who would later paint in the features. The incomplete manuscript of this volume of the *Cantigas* may in its own way, then, be as valuable as if it were complete, since in it lie important lessons in the history of miniature production, demonstrating that each page was the product of an assembly-line workmanship. According to Guerrero Lovillo, at least three styles of painting can be identified as to the depiction of the human body and face.[54] Were three different artists working at the depiction of faces and physiques? Probably, but since none is named specifically with regard to this, we will never know, even though the names of three artists listed as *pintores del rey* have survived.

Guerrero Lovillo believes that the six-panel design and even the style of depiction may derive from thirteenth-century French and Spanish ivory diptychs.[55] The surviving diptychs are not the brilliantly colored pieces they must have been, but enough chipped and faded paint remains to prove that many were polychromatic. Each diptych is framed in a frieze of carved roseates or other motifs identical in some cases to the painted friezes in the *Cantigas;* moreover, each diptych is a sculptured rendition of a miracle and each is divided into six panels which depict the events of the miracles.

It is also possible that the king and his artists were influenced by stained glass windows which portrayed miracles. The art of miniature was highly developed in France by the middle of the thirteenth century, as Dante mentioned in the *Paradiso.* The Learned King might have sent artists to Paris to learn this art, or he might have imported French miniaturists. Whatever the case, the miniatures in the *Cantigas de Santa Maria* are no mere reflection or hispanicization of French miniatures and in fact resemble more closely that art as practiced in Germany.

Dramatization might have provided still another inspiration. Some of the miracles could easily have been enacted, and it is well known that Spain produced many dramatic pieces in Latin, as well as some in the vernaculars—Castilian, Catalan, and Valencian. Alfonso was concerned about drama and its proper representation, as is witnessed in his *Siete Partidas,* his great codex of law, in which he forbade secular plays but encouraged dramas of religious intent.[56] French dramatic production might have been influential. In about 1265 Rutebeuf had produced dramatically the *Miracle de Théophile,* and the *Cantigas* contain this miracle also. If French influence in art, music, sculpture and architecture, and literature might have contributed to Spanish culture, why would the influence of French drama have been absent?

Insofar as I know, no one has suggested the possibility of the dramatization of the *Cantigas de Santa Maria.* Nor has anyone else stated that certain of the miniatures contain pictures of statuary that seem to move, without being part of the miracle illustrated by the miniatures. In *Cantiga* 18, for example, the images which are no more than part of the scene of the miracle do indeed change position, and the changes have nothing to do with the overall miraculous events. In number 18 the images of the Virgin and the Child Jesus in the first and second panels are in different positions from those of the last two panels, and yet they are the same images in the same shrine. In the first two panels the Virgin is clasping the Child tightly against her face—a little closer in the second panel than in the first— almost as if she were about to kiss him, and her right hand and arm support him as though to keep him from falling backward. But in the last two panels the Child is seated on his mother's lap and her hand merely rests on his shoulder. If an artist were sketching as he watched a dramatization of the miracle, he might have caught the actress who played the role of the seated statue in two different positions as she shifted about in order to rest. There is no proof that this is the case, but it can explain the image's altered position. Or perhaps the artist sketched from a different image the second time or painted from memory.[57]

An almost photographic realism prevails in the miniatures, and this realism quite naturally contributes, sometimes actively, sometimes passively, to the narrative techniques of the miracles. Little is left to the imagination. In the miniatures all facets of life are depicted, the beautiful as well as the ugly. Angels with pastel-shaded wings minister to mortals (*Cantiga* 7), drive away devils (3), and attend the Blessed Virgin (13); the Virgin herself appears in nearly every miracle in her endless war with the devil and his minions and in her ever-present attentiveness to the needs of mortals; beautiful landscapes abound not only in the cities (*Cantigas* 26, 28, 129) but also in the country (44, 121). Ugliness in appearance and in action and deed meets the eye frequently: *Cantiga* 17 depicts a young man having sexual intercourse with his mother who is seen later casting the issue of this incestuous union into a latrine to conceal her sin; number 38 reveals a group of young rascals carousing and drinking and throwing dice; violence is the theme of another (124) when a man is first stoned, then stabbed with a lance, and at last slashed across the throat from which his blood spurts forth; a naked penitent is revealed on his knees at a font, as the priest pours baptismal water over his head. His genitalia and the darkness of his pubic hair are perfectly visible (46).

None of what was mentioned above is pornographic, but rather the depiction of events and of life for the sake of a more vivid presentation of the miracles. Each of the *Cantigas* was aimed at credibility, pictorially and verbally. Therefore anything that contributed to credibility was included.

Even astonishingly minor details are present. A forest scene (44) reveals fauna and flora of various kinds, even wild flowers and small animals such as rabbits and mice which have to be looked for carefully, so minute are they. Realism and not impressionism is the goal of the artists of these miniatures, although the latter is not absent.

Composition in these pictures has been handled with consummate skill. An infinite variety of scenes serve as backgrounds for the miracles' landscapes, seascapes, interiors, hell, heaven. Figures group themselves artistically, revealing their emotions and reactions to events (175); hands are raised in terror (4); faces twist in fear or beam in laughter (38); a man averts his face and grimaces in pain as his foot is amputated (37).

Perspective per se is imperfect but its very imperfection provides pleasing and revealing effects. Figures playing a form of baseball (42) stand too close together—a batter prepared to strike a ball in the hands of a pitcher standing much too near him, while the men in the outfield are almost as close. The reason for the exaggerated proximity is that if perspective were observed realistically, the figures would be so tiny that they could not be seen clearly. Another example is in *Cantiga* 36 where the men on board a large ship fill it entirely, but we can see them in detail, even to their features, and none of this could have been portrayed had these men been in correct perspective to the ship.

Almost always the human figure is well depicted, leading to the conclusion that live models were used. The movements of limbs, whether bare or concealed by garments, are natural and correct. Nudes, though not present in many of the *Cantigas,* are represented and carefully depicted. Guerrero

Lovillo refers to *Cantiga* 60 in whose miniatures can be seen the figures of Adam and Eve as massive-limbed and not in consonance with the perfection of some of the nude figures in other miniatures in the *Cantigas.*[58] And yet, in number 22 appears a very handsome and well-built young peasant, who stands before his enemies in a skintight shirt and *bragas* rolled high on his thighs. His arms, neck, shoulders, and torso, as well as his thighs and calves, show the play of muscles. Young gamblers in numbers 38 and 76 are powerfully thewed of limb and reveal well-developed pectoral muscles. Number 95 shows a nude man sitting on the edge of a bed in which a naked woman reclines, her lower extremities hidden by the covers. A devil in the background possesses a muscularity approaching the heroic.

In order to reach the most effective comprehension of pictorial representation in the *Cantigas,* one should examine a particular page of miniatures to see how close the visual conception of the story parallels the written form. This is an important matter, for surprisingly enough not every page of miniatures reflects exactly what the verses narrate, although in my opinion, in the majority of cases pictorial and verbal handlings are closely knit and narrate in the two media of the visual and the written the identical brief narrative. Reasons for divergences between the visual and the written in some of the *Cantigas* leads to interesting speculations. Was the visualization of a particular miracle always based upon the Alfonsine poem, or did the artists sometimes include matters not in the poem because they based their pictures on some other version? After all, many of the *Cantigas* stemmed from well-known Latin sources. Might not the artists, perhaps unable to lay hands on the Alfonsine poems when they needed them, have gone to the archives to read the miracle in Latin? Another possibility is this: the artists may have known the miracles from another source, maybe even from simply having heard them and might therefore have painted what they recalled without adhering closely to the words of the *Cantigas* themselves. But would not the Learned King who was noted for careful editing and even for many statements that he did indeed read carefully and correct and amend, have read the poem and studied its pictorial representation? And would he not have quickly noticed the divergences? Perhaps, and yet, perhaps not. When one has read thousands of miracles from many sources and in many versions, and when he himself either has written hundreds or has caused hundreds to be written, the details of any miracle, as these vary from Latin texts to those in other languages, tend to "run together" in his mind. If the Learned King was asked to look at the miniatures for certain or for all of the *Cantigas,* he may well have done so, may have seen that the events as depicted by the artists were in general the events in the poem, without noting minor discrepancies. He might even have planned with the artists what they should include as they painted, and in this case he might simply have had them take notes on the miracles' content. If he were telling them the story they were to illustrate and not reading the *Cantiga* to them, he himself might have caused the discrepancies.

But leaving the discrepancies aside, it is time to return to the examination of a particular page of miniatures and to study its approach to narrative technique along with the narrative techniques employed verbally, with at least some brief reference to the melodic technique wedded to the visual and the verbal. Any miracle could be chosen, but number 67, because of the exceptional brilliance of its colors, the remarkable settings and characterizations, and its method of animating the story, seems a perfect choice. Moreover, its plot is unique and its denouement exceptionally well approached and presented. The subject, devil possession and exorcism, has a universal and ageless quality, and in the thirteenth century possession and the exorcism of the devil and of evil spirits were living phenomena in people's minds. The brief introductory statement which precedes number 67 makes it clear what is to follow: Como Santa Maria fez connoçer ao ome bõo que tragia o demo consigo por sergente; e quisera-o matar, senon pola oraçon que dezia." These lines can be considered a statement of the miracle's motif or of its barest plot summary.

Further summarization is next provided in the six captions, one for each of the six panels of miniatures. These captions provide at the very least a more detailed plot summary or explanation of the story. For *Cantiga* 67 they read as follows: "Como un omne bõo fez un espital e servia senpre el et seos omnes os pobres; Como el omne bõo collia omnes a soldada pera servir os pobres; Como o demo se meteu en un corpo d'omne morto e entrou con o omne bõo a soldada; Como o demo fazia a seu amo yr a monte e pescar no mar por fazerlo morrer; Como un bispo que era ospede do omne bõo connoceu aquel mao sergente; Como o bispo fez fogir o demo e o corpo en que andava caeu ant' eles.''

So far, two presentations of the miracle have appeared: the title of the miracle which is a one-sentence statement of its content and the six captions explaining the six panels of miniatures. The title and the combined captions are in essence brief narratives.

The plot in its full treatment unfolds in the poem itself, and the illustrations relate the story visually. It seems pertinent, therefore, in the interest of studying narrative techniques to investigate the visual and the written narration as these complement one another.

Since only six panels are required to illustrate the happenings in twenty stanzas of four lines and a refrain, not every detail of the plot's content could be pictured. Even so the artists have accomplished a surprising visual coverage.

Panel 1 depicts a scene in the hospital constructed by a good man to serve the poor. He can be seen with one assistant ministering to six bedridden patients. He holds a goblet to a sick man's lips and his face is benevolent and his mien and the way he offers the cup are kind. The first stanza of the poem touches none of this, nor does the second, unless the introductory remarks as to the time and locale, and the fact that the good man is charitable, can be considered to do so; the third stanza, however, does indeed parallel the illustration. Stanzas 1-3 follow to illustrate:

> E de tal razon com' esta   un miragre contar quero
> que fezo Santa Maria,   aposto e grand' e fero,
> que non foi feito tan grande   ben des lo tempo de Nero,
> que emperador de Roma   foi, daquela gran çidade.
> *A Reynna gloriosa   tant' é de gran santidat . . .*
>
> Ond' avēo que un ome   mui poderos' e louçāo,
> sisud' e fazedor d' algo   mais tant' era bon crischāo,
> que tod' ele por Deus dava   quanto collia en māo,
> ca de todas outras cousas   mays amava caridade.
> *A Reynna gloriosa   tant' é de gran santidade . . .*
>
> E por mellor fazer esto   que muit' ele cobiiçava,
> un espital fezo fora   da vila u el morava,
> en que pan e vinn' e carne   e pescad' a todos dava,
> e leitos en que jouvessen   en yvern' e en estade.
> *A Reynna gloriosa   tant' é de gran santidade . . .*

Panel 1, then, treats material found for the most part in stanza 3 with possibly some touches from stanzas 1 and 2.

Panel 2 reveals the good man hiring three young gentlemen to help him tend the sick. Their dress reveals that they are decent and proper people.

Gestures indicate that bargaining is taking place. The caption's simple statement reveals that he is employing them, as do the first two and one-half lines, but the last two and one-half reveal more, something actually depicted in the third panel. Stanza 4 then is illustrated by Panel 2, while Panel 3 illustrates the last part of stanza 4 as well as all stanza 5. In Panel 3 we see that the devil is offering his services to the good man. Visually a great deal of narrative is covered. To understand this, it is necessary to read stanzas 4 and 5:

> E como quen á gran coita,   de compri-lo que deseja,
> elle man[n]çebos collia   ben mandados, sen peleja,
> que aos pobres servissen;   mais o demo con enveja
> meteu-se en un corpo morto   d'ome de mui gran beldade,
> *A Reynna gloriosa*   *tant' é gran santidade . . .*
>
> E vēo pera el logo   mansso, en bon contenente,
> e disse: "Sennor, querede   que seja vosso sergente,
> e o serviço dos pobres   vos farei de bōa mente,
> pois vejo que vos queredes   e fazedes y bondade.
> *A Reynna gloriosa*   *tant' é de gran santidade . . .*

In the illustration of the devil hidden in the animated corpse of a handsome man, he is characterized by the garments of a gentleman and his face is benign, making it easy to understand how he could deceive the good man; but the viewer can see something that the good man cannot. He can see the face of the devil staring from the back of the living corpse's head. The words of the poem state that the devil entered the body, and the artists depict this in visual narrative with equal force. Both artist and poet are omniscient, and each portrays the devil to the viewer or reader, but not to the innocent man.

Stanzas 6, 7, and 8 describe all the devil's machinations to deceive his employer and to penetrate deeper and deeper into his good graces. For the sake of continuity these stanzas appear below. The illustration in Panel 3 can be considered to relate to these three stanzas, even if the panel shows no more than the devil and the good man conversing about the hospital position. And, since the good man is pointing toward the hospital, by implication, at least, we can consider that the panel goes beyond the stanza and covers stanzas 6, 7, and 8.

> E ssequer o meu serviço   averedes en dōado.
> Quando ll' om' oyu aquesto   dizer, foy en mui pagado;

e demais viu-o fremoso, apost' e ben razõado,
e cuidou que non andava senon con gran lealdade.
A Reynna gloriosa tant' é de gran santidade . . .

En esta guisa o demo chẽo de mal e arteiro
fez tanto que o bon ome o fillo[u] por escudeiro'
e en todos seus serviços a el achava primeiro,
dizendo-lle: "Que queredes, sennor? A min o mandade?
A Reynna gloriosa tant' é de gran santidade . . .

Tanto lle soube o diabo fazer con que lle prouguesse,
que nunca ll' ele dizia cousa que el non crevesse;
demais non avia ome que o atan ben soubesse
servir sempr' en todas cousas segundo sa voontade.
A Reynna gloriosa tant' é de gran santidade . . .

Even though no detail found in stanzas 6, 7, and 8 appears in the miniatures, this lack is made up in Panel 4. Here can be seen examples of remarkable animations and visualizations employed to tell the story pictorially. The caption of Panel 4 had stated the devil made the good man go hunting and fishing, so the miniatures had to depict the two activities within the frame of a single panel. Since the verses themselves give no details of either the hunting excursions or the fishing trip, the miniaturists, free to illustrate the concept as they pleased, gave rein to their imaginations and produced the two scenes in a truly compelling way. The good man appears in the top half of the panel on horseback and in the garments gentlemen wore when hunting or playing games. He carries a spear and with it is transfixing a bear which has reared up on its hind legs to defend itself and to attack the hunter. The thick woodland described (*monte*) in the verses is the background of the scene. Off to the right stands the devil, human faced, but otherwise infernal, with the hairy legs of a goat and the faces of imps growing from his knees and from his shoulders. The countenance of a devil still projects from the back of the human head. He points at the knight with his right hand. Then, to indicate that the viewer is to shift his eye to the second part of the panel, he points with his left hand downward to the fishing scene. The good man is in a boat trying to catch fish and a demon is pushing the boat or attempting to overturn it. The amount of movement, the variety of activity, and the continuity of the two scenes in Panel 4 reveal truly unusual visual narrative techniques, perhaps unparalleled in the Middle Ages. The imagination of the miniaturists or of the person, perhaps the king, who suggested what was to be painted must have been great. The poetic lines of stanza 9, which must be considered as the background for the illustrations follow:

> E porende lle fazia   amēude que caçasse
> enas montan[n]as mui fortes,   e eno mar que pescasse;
> e muitas artes buscava   per que algur matasse,
> per que el ouvess' a alma,   e outr' ouvess' a erdade.
> *A Reynna gloriosa   tant' é de gran santidade . . .*

Before the material illustrated in Panel 5 is treated in verse, the poem continues with more of the devil's plan to destroy his employer, and mention is made of the one deterrent that has foiled him: the good man each day as he got out of bed recited a prayer to the Blessed Virgin. Stanzas 10 and 11 treat these matters:

> En tod' est' o ome bōo   per ren mentes non metia,
> e poren de bōa mente   u ll' el consellava ya;
> mais quando se levantava,   hūa oraçon dizia
> da Virgen muy groriosa,   Reyn[n]a de piedade.
> *A Reynna gloriosa   tant' é de gran santidade . . .*

> E por aquest' aquel demo   que ll' andava por vassalo
> neun poder non avia   per nulla ren de mata-lo;
> e pero dia nen noite   non quedava de tenta-lo,
> macar lle prol non avia,   por mostrar sa crueldade.
> *A Reynna gloriosa   tant' é de gran santidade . . .*

Panels 5 and 6 must illustrate materials found in stanzas 12 through 20. Panel 5 shows the bishop who arrived at the good man's house in stanza 12 seated at table with his host. As will be read in stanza 13, his presence has greatly frightened the devil-steward who stays out of sight as much as possible, pleading illness; then in stanza 14 we read that the bishop had noticed the various servitors and has missed the devil-steward; and in stanza 15 he learns of his efficiency and desires to speak with him, sick or not. Stanza 16 reveals that the good man sent for his steward, who came trembling into the dining room. The miniature in this panel shows him on one knee, at the side of the table where the bishop, the good man, and his household are sitting. Stanzas 12 through 19 run as follows:

> Desta guisa o bon ome,   que de santidade chēo
> era, viveu mui gran tempo,   trōes que un bisp' y vēo

que foi sacar ao demo   logo as linnas do sēo,
como vos contarei ora;   e por Deus, ben m' ascuitade:
A Reynna gloriosa   *tant' é de gran santidade . . .*

Aquel bispo era ome   sant' e de mui bōa vida,
e mui mais rel[i]gioso   que sse morass' en ermida;
e por aquesto o demo   tanto temeu sa vīida,
que disse que non podia   servir por enfermidade.
A Reynna gloriosa   *tant' é de gran santidade . . .*

Ond' avēo que un dia   ambos jantando siiam
e que todo-los sergentes,   foras aquele, serviam;
preguntou-lles o bon ome   u era; eles diziam
que y servir non vēera   con mingua de sāyadade.
A Reynna gloriosa   *tant' é de gran santidade . . .*

Quand' aquest' oyu o bispo,   preguntou-lle que om' era.
E ele lle contou todo,   de com' a ele vēera
e como lle lealmente   sempre serviço fezera.
Diss' o bispo, "Venna logo,   ca de ver-l' ei soydade."
A Reynna gloriosa   *tant' é de gran santidade . . .*

Enton aquel ome bōo   enviou por el correndo.
Quand' esto soub' o diabo,   andou muito revolvendo,
mais pero na çima vēo   ant' eles todo tremendo'
e poil-lo catou o bispo,   connoçeu sa falsidade.
A Reynna gloriosa   *tant' é de gran santidade . . .*

E diss' ao [o]me bōo   "¿Deus vos ama, ben sabiades,
que vos quis guardar do demo   falss e de sas falsidades;
e eu vos mostrarei ora   com' est om' en que fiades
é demo sen nulla dulta,   mais un pouco vos calade?"
A Reynna gloriosa   *tant' é de gran santidade . . .*

E enton disse ao demo: "Di-me toda ta fazenda,
por que aquesta companna   todo teu feit[o] aprenda;
e eu te conjur' e mando   que a digas sen contenda,
per poder de Jesu-Cristo,   que é Deus en Trīidade."
A Reynna gloriosa   *tant' é de gran santidade . . .*

Enton começou o demo   a contar de com' entrara
en corpo dum ome morto,   con que enganar cuidara
a aquel con que andava,   a que sen dulta matara,
se a oraçon non fosse   de Madre de Caridade.
A Reynna gloriosa   *tant' é de gran santidade . . .*

The sixth and last panel depicts the frightful denouement of the *Cantiga* described in stanza 20. The last stanza in four graphic and simple lines explodes the surprise ending.

> "Quand' el aquesta dizia,   sol non era eu ousado
> de lle fazer mal niūu."   E pois est' ouve contado,
> leixou caer aquel corpo   en que era enserrado,
> e esvãeçeu ant' eles,   como x' era vãydade.
> *A Reynna gloriosa*   *tant' é de gran santidade . . .*

This last stanza says, then, that as soon as the demon in the dead body had confessed, he vanished before them all as though he were nothing. Out of this one line the artists produced a fearful illustration. The devil-steward stands in the middle of the scene as the people watch aghast. His clothes have vanished, and what had been the semblance of a handsome man appears as a black and rotting corpse, the hair almost fallen away, the teeth in the grimace of a skull with the skin black and stretched taut over the bones. Out of the leering mouth issues the figure of a devil replete with tail, wings, claws, and hooves. The caption of Panel 6 states succinctly that the bishop made the devil come out of the body.

This *Cantiga*'s conflict is evident almost from the outset. It is a sustained conflict maintained until the very last line of the poem; this is true both verbally and visually, and it contributes much to the plot. The plot is tightly knit with a clearly defined beginning and ending. The setting as presented verbally is general in nature, but the impression is given of a very civilized community. The hospital, the house filled with servants, the ability of the good man to entertain the bishop, and the wealth he commands to build a hospital and to employ male nurses, all combine to color the verbal setting. And, of course, when it comes to the visualization of that setting, the miniatures far outdo anything that words could say. Characterization is smoothly and unobtrusively handled: the simple, gullible rich man, whose life-style centers in charitable works, never alters. He is deceived immediately by the devil in the dead man's body. He is trusting and credulous, giving heed to the fiend's deceitful ploys, never seeing through any of them until the scales are literally pulled from his eyes as the bishop exorcizes the demon. He goes hunting at the devil's suggestion and, if we are to judge from the actions in the miniatures, he was indeed placed in great peril as he faced the bear, and as he fished it is obvious that he might well have been drowned. But even after these near-catastrophes, he still trusts his steward. Lastly, he has blind faith in Our Lady and never forgets to pray to her. He is a sweet and ingenuous person, one most people would love and admire. His foil is the devil, whose character is vividly painted in powerful strokes—verbal and pictorial.

This devil resorts to a frightful subterfuge, the zombielike occupying of a dead body, which he infuses with a supernatural life. It must have shocked the Alfonsine audience. He comes preaching his own love of piety and charity and asks for a place to work beside the good man. He was always the first to serve his employer. The poet makes him speak and his words damn him. "What do you wish, sir? Just command me." He spent all his time pleasing his master and he seemed to serve him better than any man had been served. He chose amusements that would give delight and urged his master to hunt and fish, always with the idea that he might be killed and that his soul and even his inheritance might be appropriated. Then, when the pious bishop came, he trembled, knowing his own weaknesses, and he lied about being ill so as to avoid the saintly ecclesiastic. And when forced to confess, he allowed his bitterness to emerge with the statement that he would have succeeded, too, but for the good man's prayer to the Virgin.

The theme is visually and verbally directed toward one person's problem, the good man's, whose very survival is constantly threatened, even though he is not conscious of his danger; but the peripheral implication that his problem is humanity's problem is ever present.

The verbal style is direct, almost simplistic in its recounting of an exciting story. Not many efforts are made to produce language effects as such, although some of the verbal imagery is gripping and almost biblical. The surprising way the story closes in only two lines is a stylistic triumph. Dialogue is used sparingly but effectively.

The effect is single in purpose and the tone or mood is one of confidence in the face of even infernal peril, and this is stated at the end of each of the twenty stanzas and at the beginning of the poem in such a way that no audience could ever forget it:

> *A Reynna gloriosa   tant' é de gran santidade,*
> *que con esto nos defende   do dem' e da sa maldade.*

The melody of the *Cantiga* complements the effect and tone of the verses and the visualizations. There is no need for overly rapid pacing, since only a little of the action—the events of the battle with the bear and the danger of drowning—is violent. Therefore the *Cantiga* was set to a quieter melody, plaintive and calculated to evoke the atmosphere of a bygone day. It is simple and easily remembered and very well chosen to carry the events of the poem.[59]

THE HISPANICIZATION OF TWENTY-FOUR OF THE *CANTIGAS*

Few medievalists realize that some of the *Cantigas de Santa Maria* were written in Spanish as well as in Galician. It is true that of the 400-odd in Galician only twenty-four were rendered into Castilian, but even these few are important. The reason for scholars' failure to take these *Cantigas* into consideration is owed to the fact that they have not been made available to the scholarly world and almost nothing has been written about them. Even the manuscript had been inaccessible, since the twenty-four prosifications of the *Cantigas* were penned under the pages of miniatures for *Cantigas* 2 through 25, and no one was allowed to handle the Escorial codex. Even so, many years ago R. Menéndez Pidal edited one (number 18) and this was reprinted in the recent *crestomathy* in his honor;[60] and recently Keller and Linker edited number 24 and published it in *Romance Notes*.[61] Through the kindness of the clergy in the monastery at the Escorial, Keller and Linker were able to secure color reproductions of the entire codex in which these hispanicizations appear and were therefore able to transcribe them. The Real Academia Española has published all twenty-four together with the twenty-four in Galician.[62]

The literary and linguistic importance of these twenty-four *Cantigas* is immediately obvious. They contain heretofore unknown passages in medieval Castilian and a vocabulary of words involving matters not found in other Alfonsine works. Also they may indicate that the two sister tongues, as closely related as they seem to have been, were not so close as to preclude the need for rendering the Galician-Portuguese into Spanish. And yet even though the prosifications must have been intended as parallels of the poetic version, some vary considerably from the original. One is tempted to speculate. It is possible that when the prosifications were made the scribes did not always have in hand the Galician poems and may have had to use other versions, perhaps Latin versions of the miracles, or even oral renditions. Maybe the Learned King gave the scribes an account of the miracles in Galician. Perhaps this can explain the divergences, as such royal direction may explain why the miniaturist painted events not always in consonance with the poetic version. In any event, the Castilian rendition contributes to Spanish literature twenty-four short stories not found elsewhere in the language or, to be more exact, twenty-two stories and two songs of praise, since *Cantigas* 10 and 20 are *cantigas de loor* and not miracles.

The Spanish renditions were first described by Leopoldo Cueto, Marquis of Valmar, in the introduction to his edition of the *Cantigas* printed in 1889. When Walter Mettmann published the definitive edition of the Alfonsine poems, he printed the Marquis's description: "Al pie de las páginas, y a todo lo ancho de las dos columnas del texto unas veces y otras, debajo de las miniaturas, se halla la explicación de cade cantiga en prosa castellana y con letra de la misma época. Este comentario, que en algunas hojas casi ha desaparecido por el roce constante, solo llega a la cantiga XXV."[63]

We may never know the reason which led to the prosifications in Spanish. Since they belong to the same century as the original poems, it is possible that King Alfonso himself may have ordered them penned. Perhaps he hoped to have all the *Cantigas* hispanicized and failed to accomplish the goal before he died. This could explain the small number, since further translating without his sponsorship might have been difficult or impossible. As to the absence of a translation-hispanicization of the first *Cantiga,* any surmise is admissible. Number 1 is a *cantiga de loor,* as are 10 and 20, so the fact that 1 is not a miracle does not explain its omission. Nor are the prologues translated. No attempt here, then, will be made to establish reasons for the hispanicization of 2 through 25 beyond the fact that they are the first, minus the prologues and *Cantiga* number 1, and are therefore logical as the beginning of a monumental task.

The narrative techniques used in the hispanicizations and a close comparison of the two versions will now be considered. For the present only one rendition into Spanish will be considered. Number 12 is clear and easily read in the manuscript and is brief enough for concise treatment here. To follow the comparison properly, the Galician as well as the Castilian rendition must be presented. In general the parallels are fairly close.

> Esta é como Santa Maria se queixou en Toledo eno dia
> de ssa festa de Agosto, porque os judeus crucifigavan

ũa omagen de cera, a semellança [de seu Fillo]
    O que a Santa Maria mais depraz,
    é de quen ao seu Fillo pesar faz.

E daquest' un gran miragre   vos quer' eu ora contar,
que a Reinna do Ceo   quis en Toledo mostrar
    eno dia que a Deus foi corõar,
    na sa festa que no mes d'Agosto jaz.
    O que a Santa Maria mais despraz . . .

O Arcebispo aquel dia   a gran missa ben cantou;
e quand' entrou na segreda   e a gente se calou,
    oyron voz de dona, que lles falou
    piadosa e doorida assaz.
    O que a Santa Maria mais despraz . . .

E a voz, come chorando,   dizia: "Ay Deus, ai Deus,
com' é mui grand' e provada   a perfia dos judeus
    que meu Fillo mataron, seendo seus,
    a aynda non queren con ele paz."
    O que a Santa Maria mais despraz . . .

Poi-la missa foi cantada,   o Arcebispo sayu
da eigreja e a todos   diss' o que da voz oyu;
    e toda a gent' assi lle recodyu:
    "Esto fez o poblo dos judeus malvaz."
    O que a Santa Maria mais despraz . . .

Enton todos mui correndo   começaron logo d'ir
dereit' aa judaria,   e acharon, sen mentir,
    omagen de Jeso-Crist', a que ferir
    yan os judeus e cospir-lle na faz.
    O que a Santa Maria mais despraz . . .

E sen aquest' os judeus   fezeran ũa cruz fazer
en que aquella omagen   querian logo põer.
    E por est' ouveron todos de morrer,
    e tornou-xe-lles en doo seu solaz.
    O que a Santa Maria mais despraz . . .

Esta estoria es de commo en la çibdat de Toledo en una fiesta que la
eglesia faze a Santa Maria mediada agosto, seyendo en la eglesia todo el
pueblo que y era ayuntado, asy de la çibdat commo de otras partes segunt
es costunbre de venir a esta fiesta, que los judeos de la juderia de Toledo
por escarneçer de la ley de los cristianos, que fezieron una ymajen de çera
en semejança de la que el Nuestro Señor rreçibio muerte en la cruz. E en su

signoga posieron una cruz alta en que cruçificasen a esta imagen, faziendo entender a los otros judios que aquel era el Dios de los cristianos. E en esa ora que ellos esto fazien, estando cantando el arcobispo la misa en la eglesia e deziendo la sagra [*sic*] en el altar, oyo una boz de dueña que fablava muy piadosa e doloridamente, e como llorando dezia: "Varones siervos de mi Fijo e mios, como es grande la porfia de los judios, que al mi Fijo cruçificaron, que aun agora non quieren aver paz e fazen eso mesmo a su semejança." E el arcobispo pregunto al pueblo sy oyera aquella voz e todos contaronla de la guysa qu'el arçobispo al altar lo oyera, e mandaron al alguazil que fuese a la juderia e contase ally, o los judios estodiesen juntados, sy fazien alguna cosa contra la fe de los cristianos. E fallaronlos en aquella obra do querian cruçificar la imagen. E el aguazil con los otros cristianos que con el yvan mataron luego a todos los judios que en aquel fecho fallaron. E por esto fizo el rrey Alfonso la cantiga suso dicha en que diz:

> *El que a Santa Maria mas desplaz,*
> *a su Fijo pesar gran jaz.* [64]

Stanza 1, then, is introductory, giving the time and the place of the miracle which the Queen of Heaven wished to perform on the day of her coronation in August. The Castilian prosification is more terse, stating merely that in Toledo there was a feast of the Virgin in August. No mention is made that it is a miracle "which I want to tell you," as was the case in the poem.

Stanzas 2 and 3 tell how the archbishop sang High Mass and that as he stood before the altar and the people grew quiet, they heard a woman's voice, pious and sorrowful, say (this in stanza 3): "O God, oh God, how great and proven the stubbornness of the Jews who slew my Son, who was their own, and never want peace with Him!"

The Spanish version, before it picks up the thread of the Galician poem, inserts a commentary on the Jewish blasphemy of making a waxen image of Jesus and of crucifying it in their synagogue to mock Him and show the other Jews what kind of god he is. This insertion is not good narrative technique and is far inferior to the poem's handling of this information, for in the poem we read later a living account of a particular case of blasphemy in action as part of the narrative itself. It is only after this commentary is given that the Castilian relates the events in the church as the bishop said Mass and he and the people heard the sorrowful voice of a woman which said: "Gentlemen and servants of my Son and of me, how great is the stubbornness of the Jews, who crucified my Son, who even now do not want to have peace with him and make this very likeness of him!''

Stanza 4 relates that once the Mass was said, the archbishop left the church and asked the people what they had heard and they replied: "This the wicked tribe of the Jews carry out.'' The Castilian does not allow us to hear the people's reply to the archbishop's question, but merely relates that they had heard just what he had heard when he was at the altar.

In stanza 5 all the Christians went running to the Jewish quarter and found the image of the Lord with the Jews beating it and spitting in its face.

The Castilian relates that the archbishop sent the *alguazil* to the Jewish quarter to ascertain if they were indeed committing any crime against the Christian faith, and they caught them in the act of crucifying the image.

Stanza 6 relates the actual crucifixion of the image and states that they had to die for their crime and that their delight had to turn into grief.

The Castilian states that the *alguazil* and the other Christians who had accompanied him to the ghetto immediately killed all the Jews whom they caught at the deed, and the prosification ends with the refrain almost exactly as it appears in the Galician, along with the interesting statement that because of all this King Alfonso composed the *Cantiga*.

The failure of the Castilian prosification to catch the color and the movement of the original poem is marked, and not only in this *Cantiga*. In every case the imitation is inferior to the original. The Castilian consistently reads more like a commentary, often containing preachments not found in the Galician, frequently omitting dialogue and replacing it with indirect discourse, and in general turning an active and personal account into a report.

An example of greater divergence between a poem and its prosification can be found in number 24. The same kind of commentarylike approach prevails; there is the same lack of carrying the direct discourse of the Galician over into the Castilian, with great loss to narrative technique. In the Galician the Virgin's own word carries the story for some nine lines running through three stanzas. The poetic lines live, the Castilian are but a pale report of her words.

All in all, then, the Castilian renditions of the Galician stanzas are less colorful and less artistic. Some are hardly more than lines of bare summary, and one or two do not even reach that level. Still, they offer examples of miracles in prose and in Castilian, and they are excellent examples of how pale a summary can be as compared with the vividness of original pieces of literature.

The influence of the *Cantigas de Santa Maria* in the development of brief narrative has, as yet, not been determined, but it seems that it was significant. At the very least these miracles set to verse and to melodic strains reveal narrative techniques not studied heretofore in areas not considered as pertaining to narrative, namely, the areas of music and picture. The possibility of such influence of the *Cantigas* is strong, both as to oral influence and transmission and to erudite borrowing. The format or means of presentation of Don Juan Manuel's *exemplos* is close indeed to that of the *miragres* in the *Cantigas de Santa Maria*. Each *exemplo* begins with a short sentence of introductory nature ("De lo que contesçio a un rey que queria provar a tres sus fijos") in number XXIV of *El Conde Lucanor*.[65] How very like the introductory line of the Alfonsine *Cantigas!* And consider the endings of the *exemplos*. Each and every one ends as does number XXIV with a statement and a couplet:

"Et por que don Iohan tovo este por buen exienplo, fízolo escrivir en este libro et fiz estos viessos que dizen assí:

> Por obras et maneras podrás conosçer
> a los moços quáles deven los más seer."

The ending of the prosifications of the *Cantigas* resemble Don Juan Manuel's style remarkably. The Castilian version of miracle 12 just studied reads:

E por esto fiz el rrey Alfonso la cantiga suso dicha en que diz:

> El que a Santa Maria mas desplaz,
> a su Fijo pesar gran jaz.

I know of no other similar technique of beginning as well as of ending brief narratives in medieval Spanish, except in the fifteenth-century *Libro de los exemplos por a.b.c.* by the Archdeacon Clemente Sanches de Vercial.[66] Subsequent studies will be needed before the matter of influence can be fully understood.

Whether the Galician *Cantigas* were begun long before the first one hundred were in a finished volume around 1257 or in that particular year is not of great import even though it is a well-accepted belief that the definitive edition of more than 400 miracles and songs of praise was collected and set down after 1279. Evelyn Procter gives the evidence for this.[67] The king died in 1284. What is important is that for at least twenty-two years, that is, from 1257 to 1279, Alfonso was actively concerned with the production of the *Cantigas* and might have been interested even longer. This means that the miracles were a lively concern of the monarch and of those who gathered miracles for him from other collections or from the traditions of the people and from the occurrences of miracles in Alfonso's own lifetime; it means, too, that the approaches or the means of narrating the miracles was kept alive during those years and that the *Cantigas* preserved themes, motifs, plots, narrative techniques—in words, music, and picture—for nearly a quarter of a century, if not for some years longer than that. In many ways, then, these brief narratives, these miracles, probably affected the course of early medieval Spanish short story for nearly half a century and even longer.

Notes

Introduction

1. Paull F. Baum, "The Young Man Betrothed to a Statue," *PMLA* 34: 523-79; John E. Keller, "The Motif of the Statue Bride in the *Cantigas* of Alfonso the Learned," *Studies in Philology* 54 (1959): 453-58.

2. Stith Thompson, *Motif-Index of Folk Literature* (Bloomington: Indiana University Press, 1955-1958), motif number B331.2, Llewellyn and his dog.

3. Stith Thompson, *The Folktale* (New York: Dryden, 1951), p. 19.

Chapter 1

1. Albert Lord, *The Singer of Tales* (Cambridge: Harvard University Press, 1960). This study of modern epico-narrative poems in Eastern Europe has greatly enlightened us as to the manner in which oral presentation must have been developed and transmitted in ancient times.

2. Stith Thompson, *The Folktale* (New York: Dryden, 1951). Later editions are simply reproductions of this printing.

3. The literature in this area is vast, not only in books surviving from medieval times but also in modern scholarly studies. Only a few of the most representative need be mentioned here: Marcelino Menéndez y Pelayo, *Orígenes de la novela* (Buenos Aires: Espasa-Calpe, 1946), vol. 1; Léopold Hervieux, *Les Fabulistes latins* (Paris: Librairie de Firmin-Didot, 1896); Joseph A. Mosher, *The Exemplum in the Early Religious and Didactic Literature of England* (New York: Columbia University Press, 1911); J. Th. Welter, *L'Exemplum dans la litterature religieuse et didactique de Moyen Age* (Paris: Occitania, 1914).

Chapter 2

1. Francisco Rico, "Las letras latinas del siglo XII en Galicia y Castilla," *Abaco* 2 (1969).

2. Jules Horrent, "Sur le *Carmen Campidoctoris*," *Studi Monteverdi* 1: 334-52. The text of the *Carmen* is printed in Menéndez Pidal's *La España del Cid,* 5th ed. (Madrid: Gredos, 1956), 2 vols.

3. Ed. Florencio Janer, in *Biblioteca de Autores Españoles* 57; Ed. María S. de Andrés Castellanos in *Boletín de la Real Academia Española,* anejo XI (Madrid: n.p., 1964). The former has been used because it is available in most libraries. The latter is more accurate.

4. See Alan Deyermond, *A Literary History of Spain: The Middle Ages* (New York: Barnes and Noble, 1971), p. 70.

5. J. Amador de los Ríos, *Historia crítica de la literatura española* (Madrid: Impr. de J. Rodríguez, 1861-1865).

6. Ed. Florencio Janer in *Biblioteca de Autores Españoles* 57.

Chapter 3

1. Berceo has been heavily edited. The best editions are Brian Dutton, *Los milagros de Nuestra Señora, Estudio y edición crítica* (London: Tamesis Books, 1971), his *La vida de San Millán de la Cogolla, Estudio y edición crítica* (London: Tamesis Books, 1967), and Fray Alfonso Andrés, *Vida de Santo Domingo de Silos, Edición crítico-paleográfica del códice del siglo XIII* (Madrid: Padres Benedictinos, 1958); always available, if not scientifically edited, are the editions of Florencio Janer in *Biblioteca de Autores Españoles* 57, which contains texts of all brief narrative works of Berceo. A good standard edition is that of A.G. Solalinde, *Milagros de Nuestra Señora* (Madrid: Clásicos Castellanos, 1922).

2. See Ed. Thomas Wright, *The Latin Poems . . . Attributed to Walter Mapes* (London: J.B. Nichols and Son, 1841), and Raymond S. Willis, *El libro de Alexandre,* Elliott Monographs, No. 32 (Princeton and Paris: E. Champion, 1934), and Charles Carroll Marden, *Libro de Apolonio,* Elliott Monographs, No. 6 (Princeton: E. Champion, 1922); and Alonso Zamora Vicente, *Poema de Fernán González* (Baltimore and Madrid: Clásicos Castellanos, 1904); Albert F. Kuersteiner, *Pero López de Ayala Poesías* (New York, 1920), 2 vols.

3. Machado's poem *Retablo* was printed in his *Alma, Museo, Los cantares* (Madrid: Editorial Plenitud, 1967).

4. Rubén Darío's poem on Berceo is found in his *Prosas profanas.*

5. The substance of this treatment of Miracle XXV appeared in John E. Keller, "The Enigma of Berceo's *Milagro XXV,*" *Symposium* 29 (Winter, 1975): 361-70.

6. Richard Becker, "Gonzalo de Berceo: *Milagros de Nuestra Señora* und ihre Grundlagen" (Ph.D. diss., University of Strassburg, 1910).

7. Walter Mettmann, *Afonso X, O Sabio: Cantigas de Santa Maria* (Coimbra: Acta Universitatis Conimbrigensis, 1959-1973), 4 vols.

8. In *Cantiga 18,* for example, Alfonso goes to the church which contains two pieces of silk woven miraculously by silkworms and receives one as a gift from which is made a robe for the Virgin's image in the royal chapel.

9. John E. Keller, "A Medieval Folkorist," *Folklore Studies in Honor of Arthur Palmer Hudson,* in *North Carolina Folklore* (Madrid: Soler, 1965), pp. 20-23.

10. Dutton, p. 209.

11. Ibid.

12. In the *Milagros* as numbered, the sinners are ecclesiastics: I, pride and defiance; II, fornication; III, stubbornness and impatience; VII, fornication; IX, impatience; X, avarice and covetousness; XII, vile speech; XIV, monks committed "grave sins"; XV, cleric leaves order to marry; XX, drunkenness and fornication; XXI, abbess impregnated; XXV, profanation and robbery.

13. Antonio Solalinde, p. xxxvi.

14. Dutton, p. 209, includes a Latin text of the story of Sisannio and Teodora and her conversion by Clemens.

15. The motif is common enough, ranging from the case in which only the hero chosen by God can perform the task (Arthur and the Sword Excalibur) to Berceo's "bon omne."

16. Juan Ruiz, Archpriest of Hita (*Libro de buen amor,* quatrains 1144-50), also treats the right of priests to be sentenced by their own bishops, but in a sequence in which such a right had a reason for being included.

17. *Biblioteca de Autores Españoles* 57 contains editions of all Berceo's works. These texts have been followed, since they are available.

18. T. Anthony Perry, *Art and Meaning in Berceo's Vida de Santa Oria* (New Haven: Yale University Press, 1968).

Chapter 4

1. The best biography, the one which has served as the background for most of my remarks about Alfonso's life, is that of Antonio Ballesteros-Beretta, *Alfonso X el Sabio* (Barcelona-Madrid: Salvat Editores, 1963), published under the aegis of the Consejo Superior de Investigaciones Científicas, Academia "Alfonso X el Sabio" Murcia.

2. Gerald Brenan, *The Literature of the Spanish People* (New York: Meridian Books, 1957), gives a factual and interesting account of this, together with a valuable bibliography.

3. For example, in *Cantiga* XVIII the king can be seen in the miniatures (Panel 2 in band 3) receiving one of the two pieces of silk cloth woven by silkworms which had been cured of a disease by the Virgin.

4. Ballesteros-Beretta, 123-25, reveals that the vision was seen by Alfonso in November 1225 in the Monastery of Santo Domingo de Silos.

5. Menéndez y Pelayo, *Orígenes de la novela* (Buenos Aires: Espasa-Calpe, 1946), vol. 1.

6. Evelyn Procter, *Alfonso X Patron of Literature and Learning* (Oxford: Oxford University Press, 1951), pp. 27-32, gives considerable coverage to such miracles. See also John E. Keller, *Alfonso X el Sabio* (New York: Twayne, 1967), pp. 76-78, for additional references to folk miracle, and his article, "Folklore in the *Cantigas* of Alfonso el Sabio," *Southern Folklore Quarterly* 23 (1958): 175-83.

7. Procter, p. 4.

8. Ballesteros-Beretta, p. 1053, quotes part of the king's last will and testament and reveals that the *Cantigas* were to be kept in that church where his body would be buried in Seville or, in case of burial in Murcia, in the cathedral there.

9. In the *Cancioneiro Colucci-Brancutti,* number 409 is nothing less than Number XL in the *Cantigas de Santa María.*

10. See John E. Keller's article "A Medieval Folklorist," in *Folklore Studies in Honor of Arthur Palmer Hudson* (Chapel Hill: North Carolina Folklore Society, 1965), pp. 17-24.

11. Ballesteros-Beretta, p. 252, mentions certain painters of the king, but no one knows whether or not any of these took part in producing the miniatures in the *Cantigas.*

12. Two very excellent studies of the Emperor Hadrian are Stewart Perowne, *Hadrian* (New York: Norton, 1961), and Bernard W. Henderson, *The Life and Principate of the Emperor Hadrian, A.D. 76-138* (London: Methuen, 1916).

13. See note 4.

14. Procter, pp. 32-43.

15. I am preparing a study of the twenty-eight *cantigas* which are connected with the life of Alfonso or of members of his family.

16. Anna McG. Chisman, "Enjambement in *Las Cantigas de Santa Maria* of Alfonso X, el Sabio" (Ph.D. diss., University of Toronto, 1974), especially Chapter 5 "The Grammar of Enjambement."

17. Américo Castro, *La realidad histórica de España,* 3d ed. (Mexico City: Porrúa, 1962), pp. 380-81, 404 n. 33.

18. C. Sánchez Albornoz, *España: Un enigma histórico* (Buenos Aires: Editorial Sudamericana, 1962).

19. Urban Tigner Holmes, *A History of Old French Literature from the Origins to 1300* (New York: F.S. Crofts, 1937), pp. 33-34, 193-99.

20. *Cancioneiro da Ajuda,* ed. Carolina Michaëlis de Vasconcellos (Halle: Neimeyer, 1904), and the more recent diplomatic edition of H. H. Carter (London: Giles, 1958); *Cancioneiro da Biblioteca Nacional* (formerly Antiguo Colocci-Brancutti), ed. Eliza Pacheco and José Pedro Machado (Lisbon: Lello, 1900). For an extensive bibliography, see "Medieval Portuguese Literature" by Thomas R. Hart, *The Medieval Literature of Western Europe: A Review of Research, Mainly 1930-1960* (New York: Modern Language Association, 1966).

21. Dorothy Clotelle Clarke, "Versification in Alfonso el Sabio's *Cantigas,*" *Hispanic Review* 23 (1955): 83-98.

22. Clarke, p. 84.

23. The most definitive and comprehensive study of the Hispano-Arabic poems is that of J. M. Sola-Solé, *Corpus de poesía mozárabe (Las Harga-s andalusíes)* (Barcelona: Ediciones HISPAM, 1974).

24. Gilbert Chase, *The Music of Spain,* 2d ed. (New York: Dover, 1959), p. 28.

25. Clarke, p. 94.

26. Ibid., p. 90.

27. Ibid., p. 95.

28. Chisman, p. 5.

29. Ibid., pp. 551-52.

30. Ibid., pp. 562-63.

31. Many recordings of selections from the *Cantigas de Santa Maria* have been made. Roger D. Tinnell, "A Selected and Annotated Discography of Recordings of Music from the Middle Ages in Spain—Part I," *La Corónica* 5 (Fall 1976), lists and briefly describes the content of fourteen. The disc commented upon by Saville Clark (Tinnell, p. 62) is of great value. Special attention is called to the recording issued by the Musical Heritage Society of America; in Pro-Musica's Spanish Medieval Music; in the History of Spanish Music, vol. 1, the Medieval Period; and *Las Cantigas de Santa Maria,* The Waverly Consort, a Vanguard Record.

32. Chase, p. 26.

33. Manuscript E-I, also known as MSS T.1.I, which contains the greatest

number of miniatures, occasionally shows musicians playing instruments, but E-2, known also as B.1.2, contains miniatures of musicians with their instruments before each tenth poem.

34. Saville Clark, in Tinnell, p. 62, presents a concise but valuable commentary in the reverse side of the jacket of the recording produced by Experiences Anonymes. It is from this that I quote.

35. Higinio Anglés, *La música de las* Cantigas de Santa Maria *del Rey Alfonso el Sabio* (Barcelona, 1943), p. 11.

36. Chase, p. 17.

37. See note 8.

38. Anglés, p. 11.

39. Ibid.

40. Ibid., p. 12.

41. Ibid.

42. Ibid.

43. See note 23.

44. See note 30.

45. See note 31.

46. Ibid.

47. Ibid.

48. Ibid.

49. Ibid.

50. The two manuscripts of the *Cantigas* which contain full pages of miniatures are E-I, known also as T.1.I, and F, formerly known as MS. Banco Rari 20. The first is archived at the Escorial, the second at the Bibliotheca Nazionale in Florence.

51. Walter Mettmann, *Afonso X, O Sabio: Cantigas de Santa Maria* (Coimbra: Acta Universitatis Conimbrigensis), Vols. 1 (1959), 2 (1961), 3 (1964), and 4 which is a *Glossario* (1972). All citations are from Mettmann's edition.

52. Only one complete set of reproductions of the *Cantigas* (the miniatures found in E-I) has been published. This is included, in black-and-white photography, in José Guerrero Lovillo, *Las Cantigas: Estudio arqueológico de sus miniaturas* (Madrid: Consejo Superior de Investigaciones Científicas, 1949).

53. Charles L. Nelson, "Literary and Pictorial Treatment of the Devil in the *Cantigas de Santa Maria*" (Master's thesis, University of North Carolina, 1964), pp. 45-46.

54. José Guerrero Lovillo, *Miniatura gótica castellana, siglos XIII y XIV* (Madrid: Consejo Superior de Investigaciones Científicas, 1956), pp. 12-13.

55. Ibid., p. 16.

56. In the *Siete Partidas,* Title VI, Law 34, one reads of the kinds of plays forbidden and of the varieties which were legal and valuable. Farcical plays, called *juegos de escarnio,* in fact all secular plays, were not to be presented. Religious plays, the Nativity Cycle, and the Resurrection Cycle were the ones favored. A remarkable translation of the *Partidas* is that of Samuel Parsons Scott, *Las Siete Partidas* (New York: Commercial Publishing House, 1931).

57. I have considered this matter earlier in *Alfonso X, el Sabio,* p. 92, but only briefly.

58. Guerrero Lovillo, *Estudio arqueológico,* p. 26.

59. Anglés, p. 75.

60. *Crestomatía del español medieval por Ramón Menéndez Pidal acabada y revisada por Rafael Lapesa y María Soledad de Andrés* (Madrid: Gredos, 1965), 1:252-53.

61. John E. Keller and Robert W. Linker, "Some Spanish Summaries of the *Cantigas de Santa Maria,"* *Romance Notes* 2 (Fall 1960): 1-5.

62. John E. Keller and Robert W. Linker, "Traducciones castellanas de las *Cantigas de Santa Maria,"* *Boletín de la Real Academia Española* (Mayo-Agosto, 1974), pp. 221-93.

63. Mettmann, 1:xi.

64. Keller and Linker, "Traducciones," pp. 258-59.

65. *El Conde Lucanor o Libro de los exiemplos del Conde Lucanor et de Patronio,* ed. José Manuel Blecua (Madrid: Castalia, 1969).

66. *El libro de los exemplos por a.b.c.,* ed. John E. Keller (Madrid: Consejo Superior de Investigaciones Científicas, 1961).

67. Procter, pp. 44-46.

Selected Bibliography

Primary Sources

Andrés, Alfonso. *Vida de Santo Domingo de Silos.* Edición crítico-paleográfica del códice del siglo 13. Madrid: Padres Benedictinos, 1958.

Becker, Richard. "Gonzalo de Berceo: *Milagros de Nuestra Señora* und ihre Grundlägen." Ph.D. dissertation, University of Strassburg, 1910.

Blecua, José Manuel, ed. *El Conde Lucanor o Libro de los exiemplos del Conde Lucanor et de Patronio.* Madrid: Castalia, 1969.

Braga, Theophilo, ed. *Cancioneiro Portuguez da Vaticana.* Lisbon: Lello, 1900.

Cejador y Frauca, Julio. *Juan Ruiz. El libro de buen amor.* Madrid: Clásicos Castellanos, 1930.

Dutton, Brian. *Los milagros de Nuestra Señora,* estudio y edición crítica. London: Tamesis Books, 1971.

Keller, John E., and Linker, Robert W. "Traducciones castellanas de las *Cantigas de Santa Maria.*" *Boletín de la Real Academia Española.* Mayo-Agosto, 1974.

Lapesa, Rafael, and de Andrés, María Soledad. *Crestomatía del español medieval.* Madrid: Gredos, 1965.

Marden, Charles Carroll. "El libro de Apolonio." In Elliott Monographs 6. Princeton and Paris: E. Champion, 1922.

Mettmann, Walter. *Afonso X, o Sabio. Cantigas de Santa Maria.* 4 vols. Coimbra: Acta Universitatis Conimbrigensis, 1959-1973.

Michaëlis de Vasconcellos, Carolina, ed. *Cancioneiro da Ajuda.* Halle: Max Neimeyer, 1904.

Solalinde, Antonio G. *Milagros de Nuestra Señora.* Madrid: Clásicos Castellanos, 1922.

Sola-Solé, J. M. *Corpus de poesía mozárabe.* Barcelona: Ediciones HISPAM, 1974.

Secondary Sources

Amador de los Ríos, J. *Historia crítica de la literatura española.* Madrid: J. Rodríguez, 1861-1865.

Anglés, Higinio. *La música de las Cantigas de Santa Maria del rey Alfonso el Sabio.* Barcelona: Consejo Superior de Investigaciones Científicas, 1943.

Baum, Paull F. "The Young Man Betrothed to a Statue." *PMLA* 34 (1959).

Brenan, Gerald. *The Literature of the Spanish People.* New York: Meridian Books, 1957.

Castro, Américo. *La realidad de España.* 3d ed. Mexico City: n.p. 1962.

Chisman, Anna McG. "Enjambement in *Las Cantigas de Santa Maria* of Alfonso X, el Sabio." Ph.D. dissertation, University of Toronto, 1974.

Clarke, Dorothy Clotelle. "Versification in Alfonso el Sabio's *Cantigas.*" *Hispanic Review* 23 (1955): 83-98.

Deyermond, Alan. *A Literary History of Spain: The Middle Ages.* New York: Barnes and Noble, 1971.

Guerrero Lovillo, José. *Miniatura gótica castellana, siglos XIII y XIV.* Madrid: Consejo Superior de Investigaciones Científicas, 1956.

Hart, Thomas R. "Medieval Literature." *The Medieval Literature of Western Europe: A Review of Research, Mainly 1930-1960.* New York: Modern Language Association, 1966.

Hérvieux, Léopold. *Les Fabulistes latins.* Paris: Librairie de Fermin-Didot, 1896.

Holmes, Urban Tigner. *A History of Old French Literature from the Origins to 1300.* New York: F.S. Crofts, 1937.

Horrent, Jules. "Sur le Carmen Campidoctoris." *Studi Monteverde* 1:334-52.

Lord, Albert. *The Singer of Tales.* Cambridge: Harvard University Press, 1960.

Keller, John E. "The Motif of the Statue Bride in the *Cantigas de Santa Maria* of Alfonso the Learned." *Studies in Philology* 54 (1959).

_____. "A Medieval Folklorist." *Folklore Studies in Honor of Arthur Palmer Hudson* in *North Carolina Studies in Folklore.* Madrid: Soler, 1965.

_____. *Alfonso X, el Sabio.* New York: Twayne, 1967.

_____. "Folklore in the *Cantigas* of Alfonso el Sabio." *Southern Folklore Quarterly* 23 (1959): 175-83.

_____. "Verbalization and Visualization in the *Cantigas de Santa Maria.*" *Oelschlager Festschrift*. Chapel Hill: Estudios de Hispanófila, 1976.

_____. "Medieval Spanish Literature." In *The Medieval Literature of Western Europe: A Review of Research, Mainly 1930-1960*. New York: Modern Language Association, 1966.

Menéndez y Pelayo, Marcelino. *Orígenes de la novela*. Buenos Aires: Espasa Calpe, 1946.

Mosher, Joseph A. *The Exemplum in the Early Religious and Didactic Literature of England*. New York: Columbia University Press, 1911.

Nelson, Charles L. "Literary and Pictorial Treatment of the Devil in the *Cantigas de Santa Maria.*" Master's thesis, University of North Carolina, 1964.

Perry, T. Anthony. "Art and Meaning in Berceo's *Vida de Santa Oria.*" *Yale Romantic Studies,* 2d series, 1968.

Procter, Evelyn S. *Alfonso X, Patron of Literature and Learning*. Oxford: Oxford University Press, 1951.

Rico, Francisco. "Las letras latinas del siglo XII en Galicia y Castilla," *Ábaco* 2 (1969).

Sánchez Albornoz, C. *España, un enigma histórico*. Buenos Aires: Editorial Sudamericana, 1956.

Thompson, Stith. *Motif-Index of Folk Literature*. 6 vols. Bloomington: Indiana University Press, 1955-1958.

_____. *The Folktale*. New York: Dryden, 1951.

Tinnell, Roger D. "A Selected Discography of Recordings of Music in the Middle Ages in Spain, Part I." *La Corónica* S, 1 (Fall 1976): 61-66.

Welter, J. Th. *L'exemplum dans la litterature religieuse et didactique de Moyen Age*. Paris: Occitania, 1914.

Willis, Raymond S. "El libro de Alexandre." *Elliott Monographs* 32. Princeton, N.J.: Princeton University Press, 1934.

Index